Texas Government & Politics in the New Millennium Study Guide

fourth edition

VIRGINIA STOWITTS-TRAINA

Abigail Press   Wheaton, IL 60189

Design and Production: Abigail Press
Typesetting: Abigail Press
Typeface: AGaramond
Cover Art: Sam Tolia

Texas Government & Politics in the New Millennium Study Guide
Printed in the United States of America
Translation rights reserved by the authors
Fourth Edition, 2023
ISBN 979-8-9857619-5-5

TABLE OF CONTENTS

Chapter One - A Brief Historical and Cultural Overview of Texas

CHAPTER SUMMARY: This chapter is a brief overview of the major historical events and the role individuals have played in both the historical and cultural development of Texas.

IDENTIFICATION: Briefly describe each term or the significance of the individual or the event.

Frontier Thesis

Peninsulars

Alcade

Progressive Era

Social Darwinism

Imperial Colonization Law (1823)

Manifest Destiny

Cluster Migration

Empresario System

Hasinai Confederacies

Corpus Christi de la Iseta

Tidelands

Yanaguana

TRUE/FALSE: Indicate whether each statement is true (T) or false (F). The correct answers are given at the end of the study guides.

_____1.   In the 1950s, the political tensions over the ownership of off-shore oil deposits in the Gulf of Mexico commonly known as the Tidelands caused a solid-Democratic state to vote for the Republican presidential candidate – Dwight D. Eisenhower.

_____2.   Major Native American tribes in Texas included the Caddo, Apaches and Comanches.

_____3.   Texas received its name from the Comanche Indians.

_____4.   In the early 1900s, Texas became a pioneer progressive state by passing laws regulating business trusts, outlawing child labor, regulating railroads operating in the state, addressing employer abuse concerns, and enacting reform measures for the state's prison system, the political party nomination process and insurance companies operating in Texas.

_____5.   The Alamo fell to Santa Anna's forces on March 6, 1836.

_____6.   The presidio was the military garrison assigned to a mission.

_____7.   The first Spanish fort built in Texas was Mission San Francisco de las Tejas located in East Texas.

_____8.   The era of the open cattle range came to an end with the invention of barbed wire.

_____9.   According to the provisions of the Treaty of Guadalupe Hidalgo, Texas received official recognition of its independence from Mexico, and the United States acquired the New Mexico territory and upper California for $15 million.

_____10.   The famous Chisholm Trail began in South Texas and went through modern-day Austin, Lampasses and Fort Worth before reaching its final destination in Caldwell, Kansas.

_____11.   Stephen F. Austin and others received large land grants from initially the Spanish government under the vaquero system.

_____12.   Catching Santa Anna's troops off guard, Sam Houston won the Battle of San Jacinto and ended the Texas Revolution in eighteen minutes.

_____13.   The Texas Revolution was fought over differences between the colonists and the Mexican government concerning slavery, the collection of customs and duties, and the future immigration of Anglo-Americans to the area.

_____14.   In 1685, French explorer La Salle established the first fort in Texas known as Fort St. Belle.

_____15. Texas was admitted into the United States union as the 27th state.

_____16. The Mexican government allocated to American settlers 640 acres to the head of the family, 320 acres for his wife and each child, and 80 acres for each slave.

_____17. After the Texas Revolution, most Texans favored an independent Texas rather than requesting admission to join the United States as a state.

_____18. The Texas Revolution began on October 2, 1835 in Goliad over the ownership of a cannon loaned to the settlement by the Mexican government.

_____19. The purposes of the mission system was to convert Indians to Christianity, teach them to be loyal subjects to the Spanish monarchy, and extend the authority of the Spanish government in Texas.

_____20. Under the empresario system, the owner of the land was totally responsible for providing the colonists with basic services to include military protection from hostile Indians.

_____21. The Spanish explorer Cabeza de Vaca led the search for the Seven Cities of Cibola.

_____22. The late Barbara Jordan was the first African-American woman from Texas to be elected to the United States Senate.

_____23. To be readmitted into the Union, former Confederate states had to officially recognize the 13th, 14th and 15th Amendments to the United States Constitution.

_____24. Scalawags were Northerners coming to the South during Reconstruction while carpetbaggers were Southerners sympathetic to the North.

_____25. Col. James Fannin was commander of the ill-fated garrison of Texas soldiers located in Gonzales.

_____26. Originally named Mission San Francisco Solano, Mission San Antonio de Valero (The Alamo) was relocated from El Paso to San Antonio.

_____27. Members of the Coronado Expedition were the first Europeans to see the Grand Canyon.

_____28. The Texas Rangers were founded by Governor Sam Houston in 1821.

_____29. The Sedalia and Baxter Springs Trail began in Bandera and ended in Ogallala, Nebraska.

FILL-IN-THE-BLANKS: Write the appropriate word(s) to complete the sentence. The correct answers are given at the end of study guides.

1. A Coahiciltecan tribe, the _____ settled along the banks of the San Pedro Springs located in San Antonio.

2. Although later invalidated, the _____ called for the official recognition of Texas's independence from Mexico and established the Rio Grande as the international boundary line separating the two.

3. The two primary artillery pieces of Sam Houston's Texas Revolutionary Army were affectionately known as the _____.

4. _____ formed the Second Company of Texas Volunteers who played a key role in the defeat of Santa Anna at San Jacinto.

5. Lead by Benjamin Franklin Terry, _____ fought with distinction on the Civil War battlefields of Kentucky and Tennessee.

6. Irish settlers founded the coastal bend cities of _____ and _____.

7. Beginning with Reconstruction, the southern states to include Texas passed a series of laws collectively known as the _____ to prohibit African Americans from gaining political, social and economic freedoms.

8. Although originally granted to his father, _____, the Father of Texas, brought the first Anglo-American settlers to Texas.

9. The Texas Railroad Commission was founded by former state Attorney General and later Governor of Texas _____.

10. _____ was granted a land grant to bring 400 Catholic families to Texas.

11. The late Senator _____ was the first Republican elected to the United States Senate from Texas.

12. The _____ established the primary election as the tool for political parties to select their candidates for general elections.

13. President _____ officially signed a congressional resolution in 1845 granting statehood to Texas.

14. Known as the _____, thousands of Texans fled to East Texas in fear of Santa Anna's advancing forces.

15. The foundation of the famous King Ranch was the _____ land grant, located approximately forty miles southwest of Corpus Christi.

16. In colonial Texas, a _____ was a person of mixed Spanish and Indian ancestry while a person of Mexican ancestry born in Texas was known as a _____.

17. In 1519, _____ landed his four small ships with three hundred crew members at the mouth of the Rio Grande.

18. Sam Houston used the _____ strategy against Santa Anna's advancing forces.

19. The first Czech settlement in Texas was located at _____ while _____ is the oldest Polish settlement in both Texas and the United States.

20. Commonly known as the Alamo, _____ was built near the banks of the San Antonio River in 1718.

21. _____ attempted to free Texas from Mexico by joining forces with the Cherokee Indians.

22. The common-law wife of one of Santa Anna's captains, _____ is known as the Florence Nightingale of Texas.

23. Henri Castro brought several _____ settlers to Texas to found the city of Castroville.

24. At the a convention held in Washington-on-the-Brazos on March 2, 1836, provisional governor _____, declared on Texas's independence from Mexico.

25. In 1731, fifty-five colonists from the _____ known as the Islenos settled in Villa de Bexar.

26. Led by Jose Bernardo Gutierrez and _____, the Republican Army of the North tried unsuccessfully in 1821 to seize Texas from Spanish rule.

27. The first election held for the Republic of Texas resulted in the election of _____ as its president and _____ as the vice president.

28. Under the _____, the Mexican government forbade further American immigration into Texas.

29. The _____ trail ran from Fort Concho, Texas to Cheyenne, Wyoming.

ESSAY QUESTIONS:

1. What was the impact of the Spanish mission system in the development of Texas? In your opinion, was it a success or a failure?

2. What were the causes of the Texas Revolution against Mexican rule?

3. What roles did Ben Milam, Juan Seguin, Jose Antonio Navarro and Francisco Ruiz play in the Texas Revolution?

CHAPTER TWO - Interest Groups

CHAPTER SUMMARY: This chapter examines the development of interest groups and the role they play in Texas politics and the development of public policy initiatives.

IDENTIFICATION: Briefly describe each term or the significance of the individual or the event.

Interlocking Directorate

Single Issue Groups

Networking

League of United Latin American Citizens (LULAC)

United Farm Workers Union

Democracy in America

The 8F Group

New Politics Movement

Solidary Benefits

Grassroots Organizations

Corrupt Practices Act

Citizens United v FEC

Interest Group Liberalism

Buchanan v Warley

Patronage

The Progressive Era

Spindletop

Political Action Committees

TRUE/FALSE QUESTIONS: Indicate whether each statement is true (T) or false (F). The correct answers are given at the end of the study guides.

_____ 1.   The elite theory assumes that within the public arena there will be countervailing centers of power within the governmental institutions and among outsiders.

_____ 2.   The United States Chamber of Commerce is an example of a pressure group in that it seeks to influence the policies and practices of government.

_____ 3.   By joining a group, an individual may be able to realize a private purposive incentive by the personal satisfaction of contributing to a worthy goal or purpose.

_____ 4.   After the assassination of Abraham Lincoln, Congress enacted the Civil Service Reform Act commonly known as the Pendleton Act to establishing the modern-day civil service system.

_____ 5.   The Political Activities Act of 1939, commonly known as the Hatch Act, authorized the creation of political action committees.

_____ 6.   Direct lobbying activities include assisting a legislator in drafting a bill, making personal visits to a legislator's office, or testifying at legislative hearings.

_____ 7.   An ultra-liberal organization, the John Birch Society is dedicated to fighting communism and communist influences in American life.

_____ 8.   In Texas, the Texas Abortion Rights Action League (TARAL) is the leading advocacy group in support of the Supreme Court's ruling in *Guinn v United States* upholding a woman's right to an elective abortion.

_____ 9.   The McCain-Feingold Act bans the airing of any campaign commercial using the candidate's name within 60 days of a general election.

_____ 10. Passed in 1946, the Regulation of Lobbying Act requires that all individuals participating in paid lobbying activities at the national level must file with federal authorities and submit periodic reports.

_____ 11. The Labor Management Act commonly known as the Roosevelt-Simpson Act allows states under its section 14B to choose whether or not to allow unions to organize workers in their states.

_____ 12. In *Federalist #10*, Alexander Hamilton wrote that the public good is disregarded in the conflicts of rival parties.

_____ 13. A political party is an organized collection of individuals who are bound together in shared attitudes or concerns and who makes demands on the political institutions in order to realize goals which they are unable to achieve on their own.

_____ 14. According to Texas law, registered lobbyists are prohibited from providing loans, transportation, lodging costs, and expenditures for entertainment that exceed $500 in a calendar quarter to any recipient of lobbying activities.

_____ 15. The nation's first attempt to organize workers was a secret society formed in 1869 called the American Federation of Labor.

_____ 16. The Corrupt Practices Act limits and regulates the amounts and sources of both campaign contributions and expenditures, and bars contributions from labor organizations to any federal election campaign.

_____ 17. The Federal Elections Campaign Act limits individual contributions to a maximum of $1,000 for a candidate in a national primary or general election with a $25,000 limit on any person's total contributions during an election year.

_____ 18. Both the NAACP and the ACLU have successfully used litigation to accomplish their bottom-line issues.

_____ 19 In *Federal Elections Commission v National Conservative Political Action*, the United States Supreme Court ruled that a section of the Presidential Election Campaign Fund Act limiting spending by a political action committee to $1,000 for a presidential candidate was a violation of the 1st Amendment.

_____ 20 Far too often, legislative houses experience hyperpluralism between competing groups, resulting in legislative impasses.

_____ 21. A non-union worker can realize material benefits such as better salary treatment or improved working conditions even though he/she is not a member of the union organization.

_____ 22. The American Farm Bureau Federation represents the interests of the nation's small-acre farms and ranches while the National Farmers Organization represents large-acre farms and ranches.

_____ 23. Many local interests groups fall into the category of nationally affiliates groups since they are controlled by a national organization.

_____24. Many interest groups use networking whereby several groups with similar goals and objectives meet periodically to exchange ideas and strategies.

_____25. In *The Power Elite*, C. Wright Mills contends that the United States government is controlled by a political, business and military elite that despite democracy, actually controls the decision making process.

_____26. According to Davie Truman, the capitalist theory assumes that within a public arena there will be countervailing centers of power within governmental institutions as well as outsiders.

_____27. The New Politics Movement of the 1970s and Common Cause are prime examples of public interest groups.

_____28. In 1901, Marion B. Fenwick founded the Tuesday Musical Club in San Antonio.

_____29. The San Antonio Conservation Society was founded in 1924 by Emily Edwards and Rena Maverick Green.

FILL-IN-THE-BLANK QUESTIONS: Write the appropriate word(s) to complete the sentence. The correct answers are given at the end of study guides.

1. _____ are organizations created to seek benefits on behalf of persons who are in some way incapacitated or otherwise unable to represent their own interests.

2. _____ is the view that competition and the subsequent negotiation and bargaining among multiple centers of power is the key to understanding how decisions are made.

3. In 1881, _____ founded the American Federation of Trade and Labor Unions which changed its name to the American Federation of Labor (AFL) in 1886.

4. _____ are interest groups that collect money from their members and contribute these funds to candidates and parties.

5. A _____ is a person usually acting as an agent for a pressure group, who seeks to bring about the passage or defeat of legislative bills or to influence their contents.

6. _____ is the giving or offering of anything of value with the intent of unlawfully influencing an official in the discharge of his/her duties.

7. A _____ is an interest group that advocates for the entire broad spectrum of its constituency.

8. In Texas, lobbyists operating at the state-level must register with the_____.

9. The National Association for the Advancement of Colored Persons (NAACP) was founded in 1909 by ___ _____.

10. _____ is the process of bringing together the concerns of diverse groups into a workable program.

11. _____ is bargaining on behalf of a group or employees as opposed to individual bargaining, where each worker represents him/herself.

12. _____ is the ability to gain the attention and to influence the decisions of key political agents.

13. The term _____ refers to the freezing of action on an issue as a result of the sometimes overly effective operation of the separation of powers and the checks and balances system provided by the U.S. Constitution and the natural functioning of the two-party system.

14. The _____ scandal of 1824 resulted in the United States Congress passing the Corrupt Practices Act which limited campaign contributions.

15. Awards, perks and the benefits association with membership in an interest group are collectively known as _____ .

16. _____ is the view that political power and the ability to influence the most important policy decisions is held by a few individuals who derive power from their leadership positions in large institutions.

17. A _____ is an individual who does not belong to an organized group, such as a union or a political party, but who nevertheless benefits from its activities.

18. Grassroots or _____ is influencing government decision makers through pressure usually in the form of letters, postcards, telegrams, and phone calls from a large number of constituents.

19. In 1891, two socially prominent San Antonio women founded the _____ _____ dedicating this organization to the preservation of the Alamo.

20. Founded in 1894, the _____ is the Chicago-based professional organization for city engineers and other involved in construction, management and maintenance of public works projects.

21. In *The End of Liberalism*, political scientist Theodore Lowi believed that the interplay among interest groups and government institution is basically _____ .

22. Founded in 1929 in Corpus Christi, the _____ _____ continues to be the preeminent advocate for Hispanic community.

23. A nationally-affiliated organization, the Order of the Patrons of Husbandry or the _____ _____ was founded by Oliver Kelly in 1867.

24. Founded in 1900, the _____ was founded by businessmen advocating government regulation of business practices as well as better employee working conditions.

25. _____ is a governing situation wherein so many groups so successfully compete for political power that power becomes decentralized and nothing much can get done.

26. Between 1938 and 1957, Texas politics was heavily influenced by _____, a loosely bound group of Anglo businessmen, oilmen, bankers and lawyers.

27. A _____ is an organized group that seeks to influence the politics and practices of government.

28. In _____, the United States Supreme Court ruled that the exclusion of African Americans from juries was inconsistent with the 6th Amendment to the United States Constitution.

29. Passed in 1947, the _____ outlawed several labor union practices viewed as threatening to employers.

ESSAY QUESTIONS:

1. Define pluralism and elitism. In your opinion, is the United States political process is pluralist and elitist system.

2. In your opinion, should both the federal and state governments enact legislation restricting the amount of money interest groups and political action committees donate to political candidates? Support your response.

3. What are the factors are necessary for the development of a successful interest group?

CHAPTER THREE – Political Parties

CHAPTER SUMMARY: This chapter examines the development of the state's political parties and the impact their political positions play on both state and national issues.

IDENTIFICATION: Briefly describe each term or the significance of the individual or the event.

Party in the Government

Texas Election Code

Multiparty System

Moderates

Robert Michels

Independents

Dye in the Wool

The Political Mainstream

Edmund Burke

Platform Committee

Political Spectrum

Libertarian Party

TRUE/FALSE QUESTIONS: Indicate whether each statement is true (T) or false (F). The correct answers are given at the end of study guides.

_____ 1.   Nations such as Norway and Sweden use a conflictual party system.

_____ 2.   The relationship between the various levels of the nation's two major political parties can be best described as stratarchy, with each level acting independent of each other.

_____ 3.   The term party in the electorate refers to those who identify with the party.

_____ 4.   Following the criticism of backroom politics of the 1970 National Democratic Convention, a special commission headed by Hubert Humphrey advocated a more open or grassroots convention process.

_____ 5.   Incrementalism is a doctrine holding that change in a political system occurs only by small steps each of which should be carefully evaluated before proceeding to the next step.

_____ 6.   The agenda of the new-left movement advocates a limited role for government in all policy areas to include the economy, welfare programs, the environment, and traditional moral values.

_____ 7.   The term social contract means that an individual who enjoys some benefit from living in a particular country, therefore, acknowledging its right to govern.

_____ 8.   Sterling Ross was the first Republican elected to the governorship since Reconstruction.

_____ 9.   An ideologue is an individual who believes intensely on certain political beliefs.

_____ 10.   At a political party convention, it is the responsibility of the Rules Committee to determine the process of certifying an official delegation.

_____ 11.   One of the major highlights of any political party convention, the keynote address is usually delivered by the party's rising star.

_____ 12.   In the 1950s, a splinter group of the Democratic Party called the Dixiecrats formed in protest against the Democratic Party's anti-civil rights positions.

_____ 13.   The Rules Committee establishes the official seating of convention delegates.

_____ 14.   Prescription is the action of laying down authoritative rules or directions.

_____ 15.   Alexander Hamilton's Federalist Party represented the agriculture interests of the nation while Jefferson's party articulated the issues of the emerging industrial sector.

_____ 16.   The precinct is the lowest level of the political party structure.

_____ 17.   The New Left formed in the 1960s, challenged the established political, social and economic order of the nation.

_____18. In his *Spirit of the Laws*, John Locke draws a distinction between positive liberty, which is to force someone to be free and negative liberty, which frees an individual to make his/her choice of his/her own security.

_____19. In Texas, James Hogg was the leader of both the Populist and Progressive movement.

_____20. Tacit consent means that an individual who enjoys some benefit from living in a particular country consents to obey the rules of that country, therefore, acknowledging its right to govern.

_____21. The political agenda of the La Raza Unida Party include promotion of civil rights and bilingual and bicultural education programs for Chicanos.

_____22. According to John Locke, liberty in a state is the power to do what one should want to do and without being constrained to do what one should not want to do.

_____23. Both major political parties in Texas hold their state conventions in odd-numbered years.

_____24. The modern Republican Party is the nation's only third party movement that evolved into a major political party.

_____25. The origin of the modern political party actually began in the 1660s when Thomas Osborne, the Duke of Danbury founded the Whig Party (the pro-king group) and Anthony Ashley-Cooper, the Earl of Shaftesbury founded the Tory Party (the anti-king group).

_____26. Texas Republicans oftentimes call themselves the boll weevils since they support the conservative issues of their political party.

_____27. In 2012, the Green Party ran Jill Stein for the presidency and David Collins for a seat in the United States House of Representatives.

FILL-IN-THE-BLANK QUESTIONS: Write the appropriate word(s) to complete the sentence. The correct answers are given at the end of study guides.

1. Technically, the party out power is known as the _____.

2. A political party's _____ is a statement of principles and objectives espoused by the party membership.

3. The formal _____ refers to the party professionals who run the party at the national, state and local levels.

4. _____ is the political outlook which springs from a desire to conserve existing things, held to be either good in themselves, are at least safe, familiar, and be objects of trust and affection.

5. Originally _____ was a political doctrine that espoused freedom of the individual from interference by the state, toleration by the state in matters of morality and religion, laissez-faire economic policies, and a belief in natural rights.

6. The term _____ refers to southern Democrats in the US House of Representatives who support conservative policies.

7. President _____ changed the philosophical positions of the Democratic Party which enabled President Franklin Roosevelt to implement the New Deal legislation to address the hardships caused by the Great Depression.

8. In the 1840s, a national third party movement known as the _____advocated strong anti-immigrant policies and the prohibiting Catholics and any foreign-born residents of the United States from holding public office.

9. Mario Compean and Jose Angel Gutierrez are the founding fathers of the _____.

10. Formed in 1891, the _____ was the nation's most viable third party movement.

11. In 1972, _____ ran for governor as a candidate of the La Raza Unida Party.

12. An _____ is a comprehensive system of political beliefs about the nature of people and society.

13. The _____ underscores that in every organization, whether it be a political party, a professional union, or any other association, the aristocratic tendency manifests itself very clearly.

14. A _____ is a political group or clique that functions within a larger group, such as a government, party, or organization.

15. A _____ is an organization whose members are sufficiently homogeneous to band together for the overt purpose of winning elections which entitles them to exercise government power in order to enjoy the influence, prerequisites, and advantages of authority.

16. The Texas Democratic Party uses an unique approach called the _____to select delegates to the party's presidential delegates to the national convention.

17. _____ is based on support for traditional western Judeo-Christian values not just as a matter of comfort and faith, but out of a firm belief that the secular, the economic, and the political success of the western world is rooted in this value.

18. A _____ is an individual or political group advocating a moderate approach to political decision making and to the solution of social problems.

19. _____ is defined as the political, economic and social concept that places primary emphasis on the worth, freedom and well-being of the individual rather than on the group, society, or nation.

20. A _____ is a temporary political party that often arises during a presidential election year to affect the fortunes of the two major parties.

21. The political agenda of the _____ focused on making more money available for the growing middle class and the poor.

22. Failing to win the Republican Party's presidential nomination, _____ _____ split from the party and ran as a third party candidate from the Bull Moose Party.

23. In _____, the United States Supreme Court ruled that only the credentials committee of a national political party has the authority to settle credential disputes between rival state delegations.

24. In the _____ party system the parties commanding most of the legislative seats are not too far apart on policies and have a reasonable amount of trust in each other and in the political system.

25. Alexander Hamilton is credited with founding the _____while Thomas Jefferson founded the _____, the forerunner of the modern Democratic Party.

26. In _____, the United States Supreme Court ruled in 1891 that a state's party leadership could not force the DNC's credential's committee to accept a delegation that was selected in violation of DNC rules.

27. In its Statement of Principles, the Texas _____ Party believes that no government at any level of authority has the right to violate the protected rights of any individual.

ESSAY QUESTIONS:

1. What are the functions of a political party? Which function do you believe is the most important to the viability of a political party?

2. What are the primary responsibilities of a precinct chairperson?

3. What are the differing positions taken by Texas Democrats and Republicans on reforming the state's cash bail system?

4. What are the differing positions taken by both Texas Democrats and Republicans on the appropriate means of funding the state's public school system?

5. Gun control is an on-going issue for both Texas Republicans and Democrats. In their current party platforms, what policy options do both parties offer to address this issue?

CHAPTER FOUR – Elections – Texas Style

CHAPTER SUMMARY: This chapter explores and analyzes the election process in the state of Texas. The chapter also discusses the role that the political socialization process has on the participatory involvement of the Texas voter in the political process.

IDENTIFICATION: Briefly describe each item or the significance of the individual or the event.

Box 13

Black Codes

Voting Rights Act (1965)

Culture

Caucus Primary Election

Party Purity Law

Nonpartisan Election

Party Column Ballot

Agents of Political Socialization

General Election

Straight Ticket Voting

Overseas Voting Rights Act

Provisional Ballot

Jim Crow Laws

Evaluative Orientations

Judicial Campaign Fairness Act

Senate Bill 5

TRUE/FALSE QUESTIONS: Indicate whether each statement is true (T) or false (F). The correct answers are given at the end of the study guides.

_____1.   An election is the process of selecting one person or more for an office, public or private, from a wider field of candidates.

_____2.   In order to avoid a run-off primary election, a candidate must win his/her seat with a majority vote of 50 percent plus one of the total votes cast.

_____3.   In the open primary election format, the selection of a party's candidates in an election is limited to only avowed or declared party members.

_____4.   A maintaining election occurs when the voting patterns present in the critical election remain stable with the majority party winning the election once again.

_____5.   In *City of Rome v Mitchell,* the United States Supreme Court upheld the constitutionality of the Voting Right Act.

_____6.   A campaign is the competitive effort of rival candidates for public office to win support of the voters in the period preceding an election.

_____7.   The Federal Elections Campaign Act of 1974 prohibits all political activities by federal employees as well as forbids any political committee from spending more than $3 million in any campaign.

_____8.   Until 1985, Texans were prohibited under the Black Sunday Laws from purchasing any labor-intensive items on Sundays.

_____9.   Technically, absentee voting is a process enabling qualified voters to cast their ballots in an election without going to the polls on election day.

_____10.   When O'Daniel retired from the U.S. Senate, both Coke Stevenson and Lyndon Johnson ran for his seat with Stevenson emerging as the victor.

_____11.   A closed primary format is a voting system also known as the crossover primary that permits voters to choose the party primary of their choice without declaring a political party affiliation.

_____12. In presidential primary elections, Republican Party primaries are all proportional while the Democrats favor the winner-take-all format.

_____13. In a split ticket election, voters cast all of their choices for one political party by pushing only one button.

_____14. Initiated in 1991, the early voting period for both primary and general elections is a 17-day period that ends on the eve of the primary or general election day.

_____15. Sponsored by both Senators John McCain and Russell Feingold, the Bipartisan Campaign Reform Act attempted to limit both soft- and hard money campaign donations.

_____16. The use of the poll tax was invalided with the passage of the 23rd Amendment to the United States Constitution.

_____17. The term "Yellow-Dog Democrat" refers to the general obligation to vote a straight ticket for the Democratic Party, even if a yellow dog was on the ballot.

_____18. The Far Right Movement was founded by Virginia Baptist minister Jerry Falwell in 1979.

_____19. Knowledge, accurate or otherwise, of political objects and beliefs are collectively known as affective orientations.

_____20. The grandfather clause required all voters whose grandfathers could not vote before 1860 to pass a literacy test as a requirement for voting.

_____21. In *Buckley v Valeo* (2010), the United States Supreme Court ruled that a provision of the Bipartisan Campaign Act barring the airing of advertisements days before an election as an unconstitutional violation of the 1st Amendment to the United States Constitution.

_____22. In a converting election the majority party wins, but there are some noticeable basic changes in the distribution of the party membership and philosophical preferences.

_____23. In presidential primary elections, the vote determines the number of delegates each contender will receive from their respective political parties in that state for the national convention nominating process.

_____24. Running as an uncontested candidate in a primary election enables the candidate to save his/her campaign war chest for the general election where the candidate usually faces an opponent.

_____25. In a partisan election, candidates do not run with a political party label.

_____26. The majority of Republican presidential primary elections are proportional, meaning that if a candidate wins 49 percent of the popular vote, he/she receives 49 percent of that state's convention delegate votes.

_____27. Bellwether polling is a poll sampling that is totally reflective of the entire potential voters in a designated area.

_____28. Passed in 1955, the Overseas Citizens Voting Rights Act enables all active military duty members of all military branches, their spouses and qualified dependents, as well as other citizens temporarily residing outside the United States to case absentee ballots in presidential races.

_____29. Soft money contributions are indirectly given to a candidate to offset a designated campaign expense such as the catering costs for a fund raiser.

_____30. In 1924, the Texas Legislature passed legislation establishing the white-only primary, thus limiting participation in the Republican Party to Anglos only.

_____31. Cognitive orientations center on the knowledge of political objects and beliefs.

FILL-IN-THE-BLANK QUESTIONS: Write the appropriate word(s) to complete the sentence. The correct answers are given at the end of the study guides.

1. _____ is the maximum direct participation in political, economic and social decision making by interested, active and knowledgeable local groups.

2. The majority of the states hold a _____, an intraparty election in which the voters select the candidates who will represent their political party for that particular elective seat.

3. A _____ format is an open primary election that allows voters to participate in the nominations of candidates from multiple parties on the same day.

4. The term _____ refers to the technique used by both major political parties to enhance the chances of a victory for the candidates by crossing over to the other's primary election and voting for the weaker candidate.

5. A _____ is an attempt to determine public opinion concerning issues or to forecast an election.

6. In _____, the United States Supreme Court upheld the constitutionality of the 26th Amendment lowering the voting age to eighteen.

7. The_____ refers to the tendency for a candidate heading a party ticket to attract votes for the other candidates of his/her political party.

8. _____ is the pattern of individual attitudes and orientations towards politics among members of a political system.

9. _____ is the belief that one's political participation has an effect on the course of political events.

10. _____ include one's judgments and opinions about political objects and events.

11. In Texas, voting requirements include citizenship, age, and a residency requirement of _____ immediately preceding election day.

12. Individuals acquire their political culture and their levels of participation in the political arena through a life-long process commonly known as the _____.

13. The presidential elections are _____, meaning that whichever candidate gets the most votes in that particular state, wins all of the electoral college votes allocated to that state.

14. In the _____ ballot format, the elective office is listed across the top of the page and the candidates are listed in separate columns under that heading.

15. In 1938, _____, a flour salesman successfully won his candidacy to the Texas governorship.

16. The _____ (1905) mandates that political parties in Texas will use the direct primary format to select candidates for general elections.

17. A _____ is an election that heralds a new political alignment that produces a new political majority, or that indicates a long-term shift in electoral behavior.

18. The United States use the _____ or secret ballot for all of its elections.

19. A _____ contribution is a direct donation to a candidate's campaign.

20. The _____ of 1971, allows for income tax fillers to check a box on their tax returns allowing three dollars of the tax money to be allocated to a special fund for the presidential candidates.

21. The _____ mandates that all States must providing voting systems with a manual audit capability as well as provide provisional ballots.

22. In a _____ a new party wins, not because there has been a realignment in political party preferences but because the winning party just happened to have an attractive candidate or some other factor in its favor.

23. A _____ is an election specifically scheduled to fill an office that has become vacant before the incumbent's term has expired.

24. The _____ is an interparty election held to determine a political party's representative for an election office position to be determined by the general election.

25. In *The Social Contract*, _____ believes that once elected government officials are accountable to the people who elected them in the first place.

26. In _____ (1966), the United States Supreme Court declared the poll tax unconstitutional.

ESSAY QUESTIONS:

1. What is a bellwether poll? What ensures the poll's accuracy?

2. In your opinion, what measures can be taken to reverse the trend of low voter turnout in Texas elections?

3. What agent of the political socialization process has had the greatest impact on your level of political participation? Support your response.

CHAPTER FIVE – Intergovernmental Relationships

CHAPTER SUMMARY: This chapter addresses the constitutionally mandated relationship between the states, local governing authorities, and the federal or national government. The chapter also explores the impact that federal money has on the state's financial footing.

IDENTIFICATION: Briefly describe each item or the significance of the individual or the event.

Gibbons v Ogden

Concurrent Powers

Contract with America

Reserved Powers

Ex Post Facto Laws

Empowerment Zones

McCullough v Maryland

Crossover Sanctions

Partial Pre-emption Mandate

Nation-Centered Federalism

14th Amendment to the United States Constitution

Garcia v San Antonio Metropolitan Transit Authority

Categorical Grant

TRUE/FALSE QUESTIONS: Indicate whether each statement is true (T) or false (F). The correct answers are given at the end of the study guides.

_____ 1.   The nation's first constitution was the Articles of Confederation.

_____ 2.   According to Article III of the United States Constitution, the United States Congress has the exclusive power to levy and collect taxes, borrow money, regulate interstate commerce, coin money and raise an army.

_____ 3.   Section 9 of Article I of the United States Constitution places restrictions on state governments while Section 10 of Article I places restrictions on both state and national governments.

_____ 4.   The United States Supreme Court is the court of last resort for all appellate decisions.

_____ 5.   Cooperative federalism is based on the sharing of responsibilities and joint financing of programs to address citizen needs.

_____ 6.   The Northwest Land Ordinance Act of 1785 provided federal lands for public education to state governments in the newly acquired Western territories.

_____ 7.   In the 1960s, the federal government gave project grants to state and local communities to build low-income housing units.

_____ 8.   Nearly 90 percent of all modern nation-states use the confederative format.

_____ 9.   Although all levels of government enjoy the concurrent authority to impose taxes, each level of government can only tax a different commodity or a different portion of one's income.

_____ 10.   Article IV of the United States Constitutions mandates that state governments cooperate with each other in returning fugitives from justice to the state where the crime originated.

_____ 11.   In _Plintz v United States,_ the United States Supreme Court ruled the provision of the Brady Bill mandating local officials conduct a background check prior to allowing a person to purchase a handgun as an unconstitutional intrusion upon the states.

_____ 12.   John C. Calhoun was the foremost advocate of states' rights.

_____ 13.   The federal government regulates intrastate commerce while the states have exclusive authority over interstate commerce.

_____ 14.   In _Federalist #41_, James Madison expressed the need for a stronger national government that would address the weaknesses in the Articles of Confederation.

_____ 15.   Article VII of the United States Constitution is commonly known as the Supremacy Clause.

_____16.   The United States Constitution grants to the states the reserved powers of policing powers, taxing authority, propriety powers, and the right to eminent domain.

_____17.   President Ronald Reagan created his own brand of federalism commonly referred to as creative federalism with the goal of returning more authority back to the states.

_____18.   According to the 1876 Texas Constitution, county governments fall under a unitary relationship with the state government since they cannot pass their own ordinances.

_____ 19.   Today, the majority of the federal grant programs contain crosscutting regulations such as environmental impact statements.

_____20.   A project grant was a federal payment to a state or local government for a specific purpose.

_____21.   The term layered cake federalism describes cooperative federalism.

_____22.   In _Garcia v San Antonio Metropolitan Transit Authority_, the United States Supreme Court ruled that the National Fair Labor Standards Act applied to all employees of state and local governments.

_____23.   Article V of the United States Constitution is commonly known as the Full Faith and Credit Clause.

_____24.   The necessary and proper clause of the United States Constitution is located in Article II, Section 3.

_____25.   In _Federalist #45_, Alexander Hamilton attempts to clarify the confusion surrounding the constitutionally –mandated relationship between the states and the national government.

_____26.   The Anti-Federalists led the charge to ratify the newly drafted Constitution of the United States.

_____27.   The writ of Habeas Corpus can only be revoked by the national government during times of rebellion and insurrection.

_____28.   The Supremacy Clause is detailed in Article VII of the United States Constitution.

_____29.   In _United States v Lopez_, the United States Supreme Court was given the authority review decisions issued by state courts.

_____30.   According to John C. Calhoun, any state that felt that the national government was no longer fulfilling its needs could opt to nullify its contractual obligation with the United States and basically, leave the "union".

_____31.   Dual federalism is often times called marble cake federalism.

_____32.   With approval from Congress, states can form intrastate compacts with each other.

FILL-IN-THE-BLANK QUESTIONS: Write the appropriate word(s) to complete the sentence. The correct answers are located at the end of study guides.

1. The _____ is one in which the principal power within the political system lies at the level of a national or central government rather than at the level of some smaller unit, such as a state or province.

2. _____ is the distribution of power flowing from the national government to the states and from the states to the national government.

3. The federal courts were granted the right to judicial review with the passage of the _____ of 1789.

4. In _____, the United States Supreme Court ruled that a state could not secede from the union.

5. President George W. Bush's concept of federalism was called _____, aimed at moving more federal programs to state and local control.

6. An _____ is one level of government requiring another to offer and pay for a program as a matter of law or as a prerequisite to partial or full funding for either the program in question or other programs.

7. In *Federalist #5*, _____ lamented on the failure of both the national and state governments to co-exist under the Articles of Confederation.

8. _____ is the authority of government to take one's personal property for the public good.

9. According to Calhoun's _____, the American government is federal and not national because it is a government of a community of states, and not the government of a single state or nation.

10. As part of his Great Society programs, _____ ushered in a new concept of federalism known as creative federalism.

11. _____ are federal payments to states or federal or state payments to local governments for specific purposes.

12. _____ occurs when autonomous national, subnational, and local governments pursued their own interests independently.

13. In _____, the United States Supreme Court ruled unconstitutional a state law banning the possession of guns near public schools.

14. _____ or interstate relations are those that occur between equals-that is, when states deal with other states.

15. A _____ is a loose collection of states in which principal power lies at the level of the individual state rather than at the level of the central or national government.

16. The _____ doctrine is also known as the elastic or the necessary and proper clause.

17. The practice of taking federal tax dollars collected from those in upper income brackets and redistributing them to those in lower income brackets is known as the _____.

18. President Bush's _____ education initiatives gave the federal government a more active role in public education.

19. The _____ empowers the federal government to conduct criminal investigations traditionally falling under the authority of state and local law enforcement authorities.

20. An _____ is an agreement between two or more states requiring congressional approval.

21. A _____ is a congressional law or regulation that must be enforced or state and local officials may be held accountable by civil or criminal penalties.

22. John C. Calhoun developed the concepts of nullification, concurrent majority and _____.

23. The constitutional grant of power to the states is embodied in the _____ Amendment to the United States Constitution.

24. _____ are those delegations of authority that are expressly written and granted to the national government.

25. _____ is a form of governmental structure in which power is divided between a central government and lower-level governments.

26. According to _____ of the United States Constitution, the United States Congress has the exclusive authority to levy and collect taxes for the national government, borrow money, regulate interstate commerce, coin money, raise an army, establish post offices, establish naturalization rules, issues patents and copyrights, and declare war.

27. Section _____ of Article I of the United States Constitution places restrictions on state government to include prohibiting them from entering into treaties with foreign countries, coining money, and declaring war.

28. In _____, the United States Supreme Court gave the national government the authority to control shipping on the Hudson River.

29. In 1988, the United States Supreme Court ruled in _____ that Congress could tax the interest earned from an individual's savings account as well as state and local bonds.

30. The premise of John C. Calhoun's theory of _____ is that all laws passed by Congress and signed by the president of the United States must be put before the voters in a national election for approval before the laws are implemented.

31. During his presidency, Ronald Reagan introduced _____, a shift in federalism moving governmental authority and funding from the national government to the state governments.

32. Almost all federal grants have _____ attached to them to ensure that the grant recipient complies with the necessary federal laws and regulations.

ESSAY QUESTIONS:

1. What are the fundamental differences between the unitary, confederation, and federal systems of government?

2. What was John C. Calhoun's compact theory?

3. In your opinion, should the federal government place "strings" or mandates of state and local governments who use federal money for local projects? Defend your position.

CHAPTER SIX – The Texas Constitution

CHAPTER SUMMARY: This chapter examines the several constitutions that have governed the state of Texas from its formative years as a possession of Spain and Mexico, an independent Republic, admission into both the United States and the Confederate States of America to its current status as a state in the federal union.

IDENTIFICATION: Briefly describe each term or the significance of the individual or the event.

The Grange

The Civil War Amendments to the United States Constitution

Radical Republicans

Provisional Government

Washington-on-the-Brazos

TRUE /FALSE QUESTIONS: Indicate whether each statement is true (T) or false (F). The correct answers are given at the end of the study guides.

_____1. The Enlightenment philosophers Jean Jacques Rousseau, Jean Bodin and Charles de Montesquieu believed that people in any given territory had the absolute right to life, liberty and property.

_____2. Democratic ideology is based on the concepts of individualism, liberty, equality and fraternity.

_____3. The Mexican Federation Constitution of 1824 mandated a strict separation of powers between the executive, legislative, judicial branches and government departments.

_____4. The Constitution of the State of Coachuila and Texas of 1827 mandated that any candidates for office must have possession of real property of least $8,000 and be employed in a position that paid at least $1,000 per year.

_____5. The President of the Republic of Texas was initially elected to a two-year term of office with the proviso that he could not succeed himself.

_____6. The Constitution of the Republic of Texas granted limited civil rights and liberties to slaves.

_____7. Considered to be the state's best constitution, the Texas Constitution of 1845 called for a unicameral legislative structure meeting in biennial sessions.

_____8.   The Texas Constitution of 1866 gave the governor a line-item veto authority over appropriations bills.

_____9.   Under the Mexican Federation Constitution of 1824, the province of Texas was a free standing separate state of the newly created Mexican Republic.

_____10.   The Texas Constitution of 1876 successfully curbed the powers of the governorship to ensure that no governor after E. J. Davis would abuse his/her governing authority.

_____11.   The Constitution of 1869 gave the governor the authority to designate a newspaper in each judicial district as the official publication of the state with the understanding that no article or advertisement could be published without official clearance.

_____12.   The current Texas Constitution embodies the political sentiments of its time with its emphasis on law salaries for governing officials, biennial legislative sessions, a mandate for a balanced budget, popular election of all officials to include judges, and a systematic approach to strengthen the governor's powers.

_____13.   The legislative body of the Republic of Texas consisted of a bicameral Congress with the House of Representatives as the lower house and the Senate as the upper house.

_____14.   The current Texas Constitution specifies the term of office for the governor to two years (later changed to four) with a limitation of four terms of office.

_____15.   The Constitution of 1869 provided for a free state-supported public school system and the requirement that all school age children had to attend at least four months of school each year.

_____16.   According to the current Texas Constitution, the Texas Legislature meets in a 140 day regular biennial session.

_____17.   According to the Mexican Federation Constitution of 1824, the president and vice president were elected by popular election to four-year terms of office.

_____18.   Initially, the 1876 Texas Constitution fixed the salaries of members of the Texas Legislature to $600 per month and the governor's salary to only $4,000 per year.

_____19.   The delegates at the 1875 State Constitutional Convention wanted severe regulatory policies against railroads, banks, and insurance companies.

_____20.   The Constitution of the State of Coahuila and Texas reinforced the Mexican government's concepts of separation of church and state and religious toleration.

_____21.   Fearful of losing his Radical Republican majorities in the Texas Legislature, A. J. Hamilton postponed the 1870 legislative elections until 1872.

_____22.   Although admittedly a poorly written and out-of-date document, Texas lawmakers and voters alike are opposed to calling a special constitutional convention to rewrite the current Texas Constitution.

_____ 23. The Texas Constitution of 1845 stipulates that any resident of Texas founding aiding and abetting the enemy, will foreign both their citizen rights and property ownership.

_____ 24. The 1845 state constitution established a republican form of government for the newly admitted state of the union.

_____ 25. At the 1845 state constitutional convention, delegate Frances Moore introduced a provision limiting voting rights to only white (Anglo-American) males.

FILL-IN-THE-BLANK QUESTIONS: Write the appropriate word(s) to complete the sentence. The correct answers are given at the end of the study guides.

1. _____ is the political principle of limited government under a written contract.

2. _____ is the formal institutional structure and processes of a society by which policies are developed and implemented in the form of law binding on all.

3. The Mexican government enabled its governors to use a form of veto authority known as _____.

4. A _____ protects a property owner from losing their home for certain outstanding debts.

5. In _The Rights of Man_ (1792), _____connected a nation state's constitution and its governing institutions to the concept of the social contract.

6. In _Federalist #51_, _____ defended the concepts of checks and balances and separation of powers as a means to keep the governing from abusing their authority.

7. A _____ is basically an introductory paragraph to a constitution detailing the documents ideological and political framework of its government.

8. The Constitution of the Republic of Texas established a _____format of government rather than adopting the United States federal system.

9. Immediately after the South's defeat in the Civil War, President Andrew Johnson appointed_____ as the state's provisional governor and charged him with the task of writing a new state constitution that would meet the national government's mandate to abolish slavery and establish civil rights and liberties for former slaves.

10. John Locke believed that the formulation of a government was a _____ between those who created it and those who govern it.

11. Governor E. J. Davis convinced the Texas Legislature to pass a series of laws known as the _____that granted the governor extra-ordinary authority.

12. A _____ is an administrative order having the force of law.

13. A _____ is a system of governing whereby the people elect representatives to act as their agents in the making and enforcing of laws and decisions.

14. A _____ is the fundamental or organic law of any governing body establishing the framework of government.

15. In 1215, English noblemen forced their king to sign the _____, a document establishing the protection of certain fundamental rights that the king could not deny to them.

16. An _____ is a way of life of a people, reflected in their collectively held ideas and beliefs concerning the nature of the ideal political system, economic order, social goals, and moral values.

17. In *Spirit of the Laws*, _____ emphasized the necessity of dividing or separating governing authority across the various branches of government.

18. Every state's constitution embodies the United States Constitution's inclusion of _____and _____ to ensure that governing institutions do not over-step their constitutional mandates.

19. The 1876 state constitutional convention convened with a strong representation of members of the Grange who carried the motto of _____to the convention floor.

20. The Texas Constitution of 1876 created a _____judicial structure consisting of the Texas Court of Criminal Appeals and the Texas Supreme Court.

21. One of the three Tejanos signing the Texas Declaration of Independence from Mexico, _____ _____ fought along the side of Sam Houston, survived as a prisoner of war in the ill-fated Santa Fe Expedition, and served in the Congress of the Republic of Texas.

ESSAY QUESTIONS:

1. Provide specific examples of how the current Texas Constitution uses the concepts of checks and balances and separation of powers.

2. What are some of the reasons why Texans are opposed to rewriting the state's current constitution?

3. In your opinion, why do Texans not actively participate in constitutional amendment elections?

CHAPTER SUMMARY: The bicameral Texas Legislature is primarily responsible for enacting laws that govern this state. The chapter examines the legislative process and ins-and-outs of legislative houses.

IDENTIFICATION: Briefly describe each term or the significance of the individual or the event.

Edmund Burke

Conference Committee

Thomas Hobbes

Local Calendar

Seniority System

Legislative Budget Board

Baker v Carr

Politico View of Representation

Procedural Standing Committees

Committee of the Whole

Joint Resolution

Conference Committee

Reynolds v Sims (1964)

Voting Rights Act

Red Flag Laws

Sanctuary Cities

TRUE/FALSE QUESTIONS: Indicate whether each statement is true (T) or false (F). The correct answers are given at the end of the study guides.

_____1. A House of Representatives candidate must be at least 26 years of age, a U.S. citizen and met the residency requirement of two-years in the state and one-year in the legislative district.

_____2. Whenever the lieutenant governor or the speaker of the Texas House are unavailable to attend a daily legislative session, the pro-tempore or pro-tem appointed member in each house serves as the presiding officer.

_____3. Several standing committees convert to interim committees that meet when the Texas Legislature is not officially in session.

_____4. An appropriations bills creates a program, specifies its general aims and how they are to be achieved, and unless open-ended, puts a ceiling in monies that can be used to finance it.

_____5. A pigeonhole tacit is a legislative procedure that forces a bill out of committee.

_____6. All bills demanding intermediate attention to include those submitted by the governor as emergency items as well as all revenue, tax and appropriations bills are placed on the Major State Calendar.

_____7. A concurrent resolution must be approved by both houses of the Texas Legislature but not by the governor.

_____8. E. J. Davis is the only governor of Texas to be officially impeached and removed from office.

_____9. The politico view of representation describes the lawmaker who is duty bound to vote according to the dictates of his/her constituents.

_____10. Confirmation is the power of a legislative body to approve nominations made to fill executive and judicial positions.

_____11. Amendments to the Texas Constitution are proposed by a three-fourths vote in each chamber with final approval left up to the voters.

_____12. The consent calendar concerns all bills requiring immediate attention to include those submitted by the governor as emergency items.

_____13. A bill is a proposed law that either changes an existing one or creates a new one.

_____14. Substantive standing committees handle the internal process or the flow of proposed legislative actions.

_____15. Thirty-day special sessions of the Texas Legislature can be called only by the speaker of the Texas House and the lieutenant governor.

_____16. The Legislative Council's primary duty is to prepare the upcoming legislative agenda by exploring and studying state problems and planning legislative proposals to address these concerns.

_____17. All members of the Texas Legislature are granted legislative immunity, protecting against slanderous statements made by them within the legislative houses.

_____18. Casework is the service performed by legislators and their staff at the request of and on behalf of their constituents.

_____19. At the constitution convention, John Adams expressed grave concerns over the viability and effectiveness of a unicameral or one-house legislature.

_____20. Gerrymandering is the drawing of legislative district boundary lines to obtain partisan or factional advantage.

_____21. The Sunrise Advisory Commission reviews and evaluates all state-funded agencies to ensure that they are accomplishing their goals and objectives and if not, the commission may recommend to abolish those agencies.

_____22. Members of both houses of the Texas Legislature can be censured by their colleagues by inappropriate behavior, dereliction of official duties, or malfeasance.

_____23. The membership of the Legislative Redistricting Board is the speaker, lieutenant governor, governor, comptroller, land commissioner and the state attorney general.

_____24. As specified in the Texas Constitution, all members of the Texas House and Senate must officially live in the district they represent.

_____25. The Texas Legislature is called into a regular session of no more than 140 days on the second Tuesday of even-numbered years.

_____26. In 1963, the Supreme Court ruled in *Westberry v Sanders* that each person's vote must be counted equally in statewide primary races.

FILL-IN-THE-BLANK QUESTIONS: Write the appropriate word(s) to complete the sentence. The correct answers are given at the end of study guides.

1. At the start of the 2019 legislative session, _____ was elected to the speakership of the Texas House, replacing Joe Strauss.

2. In _____, the United States Supreme Court ruled that Section 4 of the federal Voting Rights Act was unconstitutional.

3. A private bill or _____ provides an exception to a law for an individual rather than trying to change the entire bill.

4. _____ are formal expressions of opinion that are offered for approval by one or both houses of a legislature.

5. A _____ bill's scope is limited to a specified geographical area of the state or a unit of government such as a city, county, school district, precinct, etc.

6. A _____ is an attempt to grab control of the Senate floor and literally talk the bill the death.

7. _____ is a parliamentary technique used by a legislative body to end debate and bring the matter under consideration to a vote.

8. Frequently used by governors, a _____ occurs when the governor appoints an individual to assume the duties of a position pending official confirmation of the legislature when it officially convenes its next session.

9. All legislative items effecting the entire state that are not emergency items are placed on the_____ _____ calendar for consideration.

10. Select or _____ are short-term bodies assigned to investigate a particular issue or policy concern.

11. A _____ is a measure adopted by one chamber of a legislative body but does not require the approval of the other house or the signature of the governor to become effective actions.

12. _____ is the allocation of legislative seats.

13. _____ are formal expressions of opinion or decisions that are offered by a member of either the House or the Senate for approval by one of both houses of the legislature.

14. _____ is defined as the action of a state legislature or other body in redrawing legislative electoral district lines following a new population census.

15. In _____, the United States Supreme Court ruled that Texas had to adhere to the one man, one vote principle.

16. _____ is appropriations made by a legislative body providing for expenditures of suns of public money on local projects not critically needed.

17. A _____ is a legislative procedure that forces a bill out of committee.

18. A _____ occurs when both houses of a legislative body convenes as one body.

19. In _____(2006), the United States Supreme Court ruled that states can opt to redistrict as many times as they wish during the ten-year census period.

20. _____ is a formal accusation, rendered by the lower house of a legislative body that commits an accused civil official for trial in the upper house.

21. In _____, the United States Supreme Court ruled that all redistricting plans had to maximize minority representation in both national and state redistricting efforts.

22. The _____ requires that the state auditor conduct random periodic inspections of all state agencies.

23. The Texas House _____handles the internal flow of proposed legislation through the various steps of the process.

24. Both houses of the legislature have taken steps to outlaw _____, whereby someone other than the lawmaker assigned to that particular desk pushed the voting button.

25. The Texas House of Representative is composed of _____ members and the Senate has only _____ members.

26. In the _____ view of representation, lawmakers feel that they are empowered to vote according to what they consider to be in the best interests of the people they were elected to represent.

27. It is the traditional practice of the governor to exercise _____ prior to when he/she announces the appointment of an individual to a top executive position.

28. The concept of "one man, one vote" was the result of the United States Supreme Court's ruling in

_____.

ESSAY QUESTIONS:

1. Explain the roles legislative leaders fulfill as gatekeepers, coalition builders and communicators. Provide specific examples for each role.

2. What is pre-file? What are the advantages of a legislator using this method to introduce legislation?

3. Define and provide an example of minority vote packing and minority vote dilution?

CHAPTER EIGHT – The Executive Branch of Texas Government

CHAPTER SUMMARY: This chapter examines the executive branch of the state's government to include the governor's office and the state bureaucracy.

IDENTIFICATION: Briefly describe each term or the significance of the individual or the event.

Martial Law

Governor Dan Moody

Parole

Senatorial Courtesy

Governor William Hobby

Sharpstown Bank Scandal

Proclamations

Governor Mark White

The Tidelands

Governor James Allred

TRUE/FALSE QUESTIONS: Indicate whether each statement is true (T) or False (F). The correct answers are given at the end of the study guides.

_____1. The Texas Constitution of 1876 created a strong executive branch to include the power of the governor to appoint his/her own executive team similar to a president's cabinet.

_____2. A popular governor, Price Daniel served three terms in the Texas House and three terms as the state's attorney general before he ran for the governorship.

_____3. A constitutional amendment passed in 1975 changed the governor's term of office from two years to four and limited the number of consecutive terms to two.

_____4. The line-item veto enables a governor to veto a specific appropriated item of a bill without vetoing the entire legislative piece.

_____5. A clientele agency is a loose term for any government organization whose prime mission is to promote, serve, or represent the interest(s) of a particular group.

_____6. Governor Mark White appointed local attorney Lena Guerrero to the Texas Railroad Commission, making her the first woman and Hispanic to serve on this regulatory board.

_____7. Executive clemency actually sets aside or reduces a convict's sentence.

_____8. Joseph Sayers was the first Texas governor to request federal assistance for a natural disaster.

_____9. In Texas, the governor and lieutenant governor run for office as a ticket or team similar to candidates for the presidency and vice presidency of the United States.

_____10. In 1994, the Texas Legislature officially abolished the office of Comptroller of Public Accounts and merged those duties under the State Treasurer's office.

_____11. The Commissioner of the General Land Office oversees the sale and/or lease of all state held public land and manages the Veterans Program.

_____12. Governor Oscar Colquitt was instrumental in passing the state's first pure food law.

_____13. The Budget, Planning and Policy Division is an executive office that assists the governor in preparing his/her plan for the upcoming budget to be presented to the Texas Legislature for consideration.

_____14. Far too often the mere threat of a governor's veto moves legislative houses to incorporate the governor's issues into pending legislation.

_____15. The governor is chief of state, the voice of the people, chief executive, commander-in-chief of the state's armed forces, chief legislator, and chief of his party.

_____16. George W. Bush was the first Republican elected to the Texas governorship since Reconstruction.

_____17. The governor has ten days when the legislature in is session and 15 days when it is not in session to consider whether to sign, veto, or not sign and automatically let the bill become law.

_____18. A commutation is an executive's granting of a release from the legal consequences of a criminal act whereas, a pardon is the reduction of a sentence.

_____19. The primary function of the state's over 250 boards and commissions is to establish the policy directives needed to implement state laws and regulations passed by the Texas Legislature.

_____20.   Both the federal and several state governments have passed whistleblower protection laws to shield those government employees who report inefficiencies and policy violations to their supervisors.

_____21.   The current Texas Constitution requires that any candidates for Agricultural Commissioner must be a practicing farmer or rancher.

_____22.   Governor Ann Richards was called upon by President George H. Bush to assist the federal government with the implementation of the NAFTA agreement with Mexico.

_____23.   Although rarely used, an address is a process whereby the courts can remove an appointee from office.

_____24.   Article IV, of the Texas Constitution states that candidates for the governorship must be at least 35 years of age, a citizen of the United States, and reside in the state at least ten years immediately preceding his/her election.

_____25.   A adamant supporter of the confederate cause, Sam Houston resigned his United States senatorial seat to run for the governorship as a third party candidate, pledging that if elected, the state would leave the federal union.

_____26.   The governor's 2017 special session agenda included a bill preventing cities from regulating tree-cutting on private property.

FILL-IN-THE-BLANK QUESTIONS: Write the appropriate word(s) to complete the sentence. The correct answers are given at the end of the study guides.

1. Although never holding an elective public office, _____served on several civic organizations to include the Cattleman's Association.

2. _____ is the only Texas governor to be elected to three consecutive two-year terms while Perry has been elected to three consecutive four-year terms of office.

3. A _____ veto is the governor's action of vetoing a bill after the legislature has officially adjourned.

4. _____ is the only Texas governor to be officially impeached and removed from office.

5. It was Governor _____who lobbied for the passage of a measure giving Mexican legal and illegal immigrants the same rights and privileges as legal residents of Texas.

6. All state executive offices are elective except _____.

7. To date, _____is the state's longest serving lieutenant governor.

8. A recent candidate for governor, _____ publically challenged Lieutenant Governor David Dewhurst and Governor Rick Perry over the state budgetary issues.

9. A _____ is the totality of government offices or bureaus that constitutes the permanent government of a state.

10. The state's oldest regulatory commission, the _____was founded by Governor James Hogg.

11. An _____ is a pattern of stable relationships between an agency in the executive branch, a state legislative committee and one or more organized groups or clients.

12. A _____ enables the governor to appoint someone to a position when the legislature is not in session with the proviso that once the Legislative session begins the appointee's name is submitted for approval by the Texas Senate.

13. _____ served as the president of the Republic of Texas from 1838-1841.

14. _____ served as the state's comptroller of public accounts prior to her election to the governorship.

15. The Texas Constitution of 1876 created the _____form of government whereby the governorship shares the same power position with all of the state executive offices.

16. In 2001, Perry's use of the veto was commonly known as the _____.

17. The _____ is the state's legal representative in any litigation involving the state of Texas.

18. All state agencies have _____ authority of rule-making and _____ functions to include investigative authority and the power to adjudicate and judge those guilty of infractions.

19. In 1998, _____ became the state's only Republican lieutenant governor since Reconstruction.

20. Governor _____ was instrumental in the passage of the Terrell Elections Law that helped to eliminated election fraud.

21. An _____ is any rule or regulation issued by a chief administrative authority that because of precedent and existing legislative authorization, has the effect of law.

22. Unlike Texas, some state constitutions empower their governors to use a _____veto which allows the governor to reduce an appropriations without actually eliminating it.

23. The current Texas Constitution requires that the governor deliver a _____ at the beginning of each legislative session.

24. Although both had no prior elective office experience, _____ and George W. Bush impressed voters with their successful oil business ventures.

25. With the resignation of Carlos Cascos, Governor Abbott made an interim appointment of _____ _____ to fill the Secretary of State position.

ESSAY QUESTIONS:

1. How has the plural executive governing format weakened the authority of the Texas governor? Provide specific examples.

2. In your opinion, should Governor Preston Smith have been impeached for his role in the Sharpstown Bank Scandal? Support your response.

3. In what ways is decentralization and fragmentation harmful to effective government? Provide specific examples.

CHAPTER NINE – The Judicial Branch of Texas Government

CHAPTER SUMMARY: This chapter focuses on the interrelationship of the police, the court system and the correctional facilities operating in Texas under the umbrella of the state's judicial system.

IDENTIFICATION: Briefly describe each term or indicate the insignificance of the individual or the event.

Adversary System

Brown v Mississippi

In re Gault

Just Deserts Concept

Mapp v Ohio

Miranda v Arizona

Palko v Connecticut

Powell v Alabama

Precedents

Remedy

Alabama v Shelton

Canon Law

Glossip v Gross (2015)

Cite and Release

Texas v Cobb (2001)

Illinois v Krull (1967)

De Novo

TRUE/FALSE QUESTIONS: Indicate whether each statement is true (T) or false (F). The correct answers are given at the end of the study guides.

_____1. Chief Justice of the Supreme Court John Marshall wrote that "the life of the law has not been logic; it has been experience."

_____2. Under the American judicial system, a criminal law conviction is based upon the preponderance of the evidence.

_____3. Criminal law in Texas is defined and codified in both the *Texas Penal Code* and the *Texas Criminal Code*.

_____4. In 1963, the United States Supreme Court ruled in *Wiggins v Smith* that the right to a Court appointed legal counsel to indigent defendants was a constitutional guarantee.

_____5. Equity law leaves a judge the reasonable freedom to other preventive measures such as injunctions or restraining orders.

_____6. In *Coleman v Alabama*, the United States Supreme Court ruled that it is not essential for counsel to be present at the defendant's initial appearance, bail hearings, or preliminary hearings.

_____7. Policing the state's highways is the primary function of Department of Public Safety Highway Patrol.

_____8. Evidence obtained that was not officially listed in the search warrant can be admissible in a trial under the good faith exception.

_____9. A felony is a serious crime punishable by death or imprisonment in a penitentiary for a year or more.

_____10. Defined as minor offenses, misdemeanor crimes in Texas are classified as either first, second or third degree violations.

_____11. A defendant accused of a felony crime would be tried in a district court.

_____12. In *Chavez v Martinez*, the United States Supreme Court ruled that the defendant's confession was admissible even though at the time of the interrogation process the defendant's attorney was unable to be present.

_____13. The United States Supreme Court and all federal appellate courts were given the power of judicial review with the passage of the 3rd Amendment to the United States Constitution.

_____14. In Texas, district courts are commonly known as "people's courts."

_____15. Noted Roman political theorist and statesman, Cicero believed that the law is the highest reason implanted by nature which commands what ought to be done and forbids the opposite.

_____16. In Texas, civil law is codified in *Vernon's Annotated Civil Statutes*.

_____17. Candidates for a seat on the Texas Supreme Court or the Court of Criminal Appeals must be at least thirty-five years of age, a citizen of the United States, a resident of Texas, a licensed attorney and have at least ten years experience as either a lawyer, judge or both.

_____18. The primary responsibility of a petit jury is to review the evidence gathered by the prosecution to determine whether or not the evidence is sufficient to proceed to trial.

_____19. Judicial candidates for all levels of courts must be licensed and practicing attorneys.

_____20. Appellate jurisdiction is the authority of a court to hear a case in the first instance.

_____21. With or without a search warrant, evidence seized during a search is legal if it is in plain view of the officer.

_____22. In *U.S. v Lopez*, the United States Supreme Court ruled that polygraphs cannot be used as court evidence.

_____23. The 4th Amendment to the United States Constitution guarantees the right to legal counsel while the 6th Amendment protects against unreasonable searches and seizures.

_____24. The two parties in a civil case are the plaintiff who initiates the suit and the defendant, the person accused of causing harm to the plaintiff.

_____25. A grand jury can either true bill a case for trial or issue a no bill decision meaning that there is not enough evidence to send the case to trial.

_____26. The term *writ of corpus* is a Latin term meaning to let the previous decision stand.

_____27. Although many states have passed similar legislation, Texas does not have a speedy trial law that mandates that trials must be placed on the court docket within a specified time period.

_____28. The trial process in Texas involves two steps whereby a guilty verdict rendered by a petit jury automatically moves to the second phase – the sentencing hearing.

_____29. The Texas Legislature has shifted the emphasis for juvenile offenders from incarceration in a boot camp environment to one that encourages community and family-oriented rehabilitation programs.

_____30. Negligence is the carelessness or failure to use ordinary care, under the particular circumstances revealed by the evidence in the lawsuit.

_____31. Small claims courts are commonly known as judicial courts.

_____32. The Texas Fair Defense Act provides state funding to state courts to ensure that all indigent defendants are provided legal counsel.

_____33. City council governments in general-law cities have the state constitutional authority to pass ordinances.

_____34. The Supreme Court's landmark decision in _Ruiz v Estelle_ mandated that any indigent accused of committing a federal crime must been provided with a court appointed attorney.

_____35. In _Minnick v Mississippi_, the United States Supreme Court ruled that any confession obtained through physical or psychological coercion is inadmissible in court.

_____36. A writ of Habeas Corpus is an order issued by a higher court to a lower court to send up the records of a case of review.

_____37. A Class C Misdemeanor offense is levied against those charged with a first offense of driving while intoxicated, and prostitution.

_____38. A true bill decision by a grand jury leads to the issuance of formal indictment against the accused.

FILL-IN-THE-BLANK QUESTIONS: Write the appropriate word(s) to complete the sentence. The correct answers are given at the end of the study guides.

1. _____ is judge-made law that originated in England from decisions shaped according to prevailing customs.

2. _____ deals with disagreements between individuals.

3. In a criminal case, a guilty verdict must be based on evidence that proves _____ that the defendant committed the criminal act.

4. In 1972, the United States Supreme Court ruled the death penalty unconstitutional by its decision in __
_____.

5. In _____, the United States Supreme Court ruled that juries, not judges must decide whether or not a convicted murderer should receive the death penalty.

6. A _____ is a written document, signed by a judge or magistrate authorizing a law enforcement officer to conduct a search.

7. In Texas, a _____ is charged against those who murder a peace officer, firefighter or employee of a penal institution who is acting in his/her official capacity.

8. The highest appellate courts in Texas are the _____for civil and juvenile cases and the _____which hears all other criminal appellate cases.

9. A _____ is an impartial body that sits in judgment of criminal or civil cases.

10. _____ is the process through which a defendant pleads guilty to a criminal charge with the expectation of receiving some consideration from the state.

11. The _____ allows a judge to ruled any evidence obtained illegally in a search as inadmissible in court.

12. In _____, the United States Supreme Court ruled that a good faith exception search was a constitutional one even though the victim allowed entry into an apartment she no longer resided in with the accused.

13. Laws passed by either the United States Congress or state legislative houses are known as _____.

14. _____ is the law of civil wrongs.

15. _____ is a relapse into criminal behavior.

16. _____ applies to offenses against the state itself, that is actions that may be directed against a person but that are deemed to be offensive to society as a whole.

17. If a fair and impartial jury is not possible, the judge may order a _____, which moves the trial to a more neutral site.

18. In _____, the United States Supreme Court ruled that the practice of overcrowding prisons was a violation of the 8th Amendment's guarantee against cruel and unusual punishment.

19. _____is the authority vested in a court to hear and decide a case.

20. An accused individual can be released on _____ based on the defendant's prior criminal record, employment, ties to the community, etc.

21. The_____to the United States Constitution forbids cruel and unusual punishment.

22. _____ is that branch of law that creates administrative agencies, establishes their methods of procedure, and determines the scope of judicial review of agency practices and actions.

23. In all appellate issues, the United States Supreme Court is the _____, meaning there is no higher level within the judicial system.

24. An _____ is a court order that requires a person to take an action or to refrain from taking an action.

25. _____ is the rules of conduct that pertain to a given political order of society that are backed by the organized force of the community.

26. Whereas individuals convicted of misdemeanor offense serve time in county jails, felonies in state prisons, juvenile offenders convicted of serious criminal acts are placed with the _____.

27. _____ is the compilation of all court rulings on the meaning of the various words, phrases, and clauses in the United States Constitution.

28. The courts of _____ and _____ are the respective state level courts of last resort for both civil and criminal cases.

29. In _____, the United States Supreme Court mandated that law enforcement officers must require a defendant to sign a statement that he/she understood the repercussions of their confession and voluntarily admitted to their criminal act.

30. The _____ replaced the Texas Youth Commission and the Texas Juvenile Probation Commission.

31. A _____ entrails the commission of murder, indecency with a child, attempted capital murder and aggravated assault.

32. In _____, the United States Supreme Court drew a distinction between reasonable and unreasonable searches.

33. In _____, the United States Supreme Court ruled that the execution of the mentally handicapped is a violation of the 8th Amendment's prohibition of cruel and unusual punishment.

34. _____ is a cash payment for release from incarceration pending trial.

35. _____ is the authority of a court to hear a cause in the first instance.

36. If the United States Supreme Court declines to render a decision, the issue can be declared a _____ _____whereby the desired remedy can be made only by a legislative body.

37. An _____ is the formal accusation drawn up by the prosecutor and brought by a grand jury, charging a person with the commission of a crime.

38. Paneling a jury is a two-step process of statuary exemptions followed by _____ _____ of those the attorneys feel would not be supportive of their side in the case.

ESSAY QUESTIONS:

1. What has been the impact of the Supreme Court's ruling in *Miranda v Arizona* on both law enforcement agencies and the courts?

2. What is the Missouri Plan?

3. In your opinion, should the State of Texas abolish the death penalty? Support your response.

CHAPTER TEN – The Public Policy Process

CHAPTER SUMMARY: This chapter examines the process of developing public policy initiatives. Regardless of the policy issue, the process revolves around eight stages with the understanding that each step must be given deliberative consideration. The chapter also focuses on the state's budgeting process to include an analysis of revenue generation and expending state monies.

IDENTIFICATION: Briefly define each term or indicate the significance of the individual or the event.

Appropriations Committees

Balanced Budget

Dual Budgeting Concept

Franchise Tax

Goals

Planning Program Budgeting Concept

Policy Outcomes

Political Implications of Public Policy

Tax Abatements

Tax Reliability

Incremental Budgetary Process

Tax Accuracy

TRUE/FALSE QUESTIONS: Indicate whether each statement is true (T) or false (F). The correct answers are given at the end of the study guides.

_____1.   Decision making is a flow and pattern of action that extends over time and includes many decisions, some routine and some not so routine.

_____2.   The root causes of a problem or casual factors that contributed to the problem should be the targets of legislative actions if lawmakers truly want to solve the problem.

_____3.   The curative approach seeks to punish those deemed responsible for the creation of the problem in the first place as well as those adversely impacted by it.

_____4.   Redistributive policies are conscious attempts by the government to manipulate the allocation of wealth, property, rights, or some other value among broad classes or groups in society.

_____5.   The federal government initiated the move towards regulation of the private sector with the passage of the Taft-Hartley Act in 1887.

_____6.   The Texas Legislature prepares an annual budget for the fiscal year beginning September 1st and ending August 31st.

_____7.   Pork barrel politics is the use of political influence by members of state legislative houses to secure government funds and projects for their constituents.

_____8.   A tax is tagged as inelastic when it does not generate increased revenue in proportion to economic growth.

_____9.   Operating expenses are multi-year or amortized costs while capital expenses are the yearly costs of running a government agency or program.

_____10.   A regressive tax is any tax in which the burden falls relatively more heavily upon low-income groups than upon wealthy taxpayers.

_____11.   The rate of a tax is the percentage of an item that is taxable whereas, the base rate is the items subjected to the tax.

_____12.   Guilt taxes are charged on all alcoholic beverages whether they are purchased from a retail store, over the counter at a restaurant or on an airline or train.

_____13.   Inelastic taxes are the most reliable and predictable sources of revenue.

_____14.   All public policies have an authoritative, potentially legally coercive quality that the policies of private organizations do not have.

_____15.   Proportional taxes impose an unequal tax burden on the wealthy.

_____16. The shortness of the Texas legislative session does not allow state legislators the luxury of ensuring that every legislative act passed during that session will be effective in addressing its goals and objectives, fiscally responsible, and administered effectively.

_____17. Action plans must include measurable and attainable goals and objectives.

_____18. A severance tax is levied for the extraction of any natural resource from the earth to include off-shore oil drilling operations.

_____19. A regressive-consumer driven tax, the motor fuels tax is levied on gasoline, diesel fuels and liquid petroleum gas.

_____20. A progressive tax is any tax in which the tax rates increase as the tax base increases.

_____21. The visibility of a tax refers to whether, given a state's economic situation, the tax is taxing above or below its capacity to raise revenue.

_____22. The planning program budget concept is a virtually automatic budgeting process whereby state agencies receive marginal budgetary increases or decreases with each new budget cycle.

_____23. Regulatory policies are governmental actions that extend government control over the particular behavior of private individuals or businesses.

_____24. The curative approach actually attempts to eliminate or cure the problem.

_____25. Policymaking involves a discrete choice from among two or more alternatives.

_____26. Pork barrel politics is the use of political influence by members of Congress or state legislators to secure government funds and projects for their constituents.

_____27. Elastic taxes are the least reliable and predictable sources of revenue.

_____28. The tax yield is not how money a tax will ultimately produce.

FILL-IN-THE-BLANK QUESTIONS: Write the appropriate word(s) to complete the sentence. The correct answers are given at the end of the study guides.

1. _____ is the action actually taken in pursuance of policy decisions and statements.

2. All government contracts contain _____ that the recipient must follow or face losing the contract.

3. A _____ is defined as a condition or situation that produces needs or dissatisfaction among people for which relief or redress by governmental action is sought.

4. _____ are the strategies used to obtain desired goals.

5. The _____ approach recognizes the potential for future suffering by providing a safety net for those who could be adversely impacted by the problem or issue.

6. _____ are governmental actions that convey tangible benefits to individuals, groups or corporations.

7. _____ is a general effort to relieve the disincentives toward efficiency in public organizations by subjecting them to the incentives of the private market.

8. _____ ensures that money will be used for its intended purpose.

9. _____ is the withholding by the executive branch of funds authorized and appropriated by law through the legislative branch.

10. Created in 1949, the _____is the dominating actor in the drafting of the state's budget.

11. A _____ is a compulsory contribution for a public purpose rather than for the personal benefit of an individual.

12. _____ is public policy that concerns taxes, government spending, public debt, and management of government money.

13. _____ involve what government is going to do, such as construction of highways, paying welfare benefits, etc.

14. _____ is defined as a purposive course of action followed by an actor or set of actors in dealing with a problem or matter of concern.

15. A _____ is privilege granted by government to do something that it otherwise considers to be illegal.

16. The _____ policy approach is designed to address current suffering caused by the policy problem or issue without actually attempting to solve the problem itself.

17. _____ are simply government grants of cash and other commodities.

18. _____ is the budgetary practice of allocating a specific tax revenue stream for a specific purpose such as allocation a certain percentage of the hotel occupancy tax to promote tourism.

19. _____ is an economic criterion applied to a tax that refers to the tax's ability to generate increased revenue as economic growth or inflation increases.

20. _____ budgeting is based on the concept that the allocation of funds for any expenditure begins anew with each budgetary cycle.

21. A _____ occurs when a state spends more than it earns within a designated budgetary period.

22. A _____ is an estimate of the receipts and expenditures needed by government to carry out its program in some future period, usually a fiscal year.

23. _____ pertains to how something is going to be done or who is going to take action.

24. _____ are specific sums that consumers of a government service pay to receive that service.

25. _____ is an officially expressed intention backed by a sanction, which can be a reward or a punishment.

26. The _____ approach recognizes the potential for future suffering by providing a safety net for those who could be adversely impacted by the problem or the issue.

27. The _____ allows the governor to veto or zero out a specific budgetary item without vetoing the entire budget.

28. Amortized costs usually fall into the _____ side of the budgetary expenses.

ESSAY QUESTIONS:

1. What are the five fundamental principles for the development of public policy?

2. What is the purpose of charging user fees for public services?

3. What were the causal factors that caused the devastating flooding New Orleans during Katrina? What can be done to minimize the damage if another category 5 storm hits the area?

4. What are the problems associated with privatizing programs traditionally delivered by government agencies?

CHAPTER ELEVEN– Civil Liberties and Civil Rights

CHAPTER SUMMARY: This chapter explores the quest for minority population groups and women to achieve civil liberties and civil rights as well as the actions taken at both the federal and state level to address these concerns. Also attention is given to the on-going problems associated with equality and human rights.

IDENTIFICATIONS: Briefly define the term or indicate the significance of the individual or the event.

1st Amendment to the United States Constitution

Brady Bill

Coates v Cincinnati

Cynthia Ann Parker

James Byrd Jr., Hate Crime Bill

John Locke

Libel

Lemon Test

Separation Theory

Smith Act

Quanah Parker

Affirmative Action

Dawes Act

Battle of Blanco Canyon

Kay Bailey Hutchinson

Mitchell v Holmes

Tinker v Des Moines School District (1968)

De Facto Discrimination

The Smith Act

Apartheid

Association of Southern Women for the Prevention of Lynching

TRUE/FALSE QUESTIONS: Indicate whether each statement is true (T) or false (F). The correct answers are given at the end of the study guides.

_____1.   Reasonable restrictions are the local and rational curtailments enacted by government upon the absolute unrestrained pursuit of unalienable rights in order to guarantee the right to do anything one wants to do in pursuit of this freedom.

_____2.   Symbolic speech is speech without any conduct.

_____3.   As evidenced in the Supreme Court's ruling in *Street v New York*, any burning of the American flag even in protest is unconstitutional.

_____4.   In *Roth v United States* (1957), the United States Supreme Court established the criteria for determining obscenity.

_____5.   Substantive due process refers to the content or subject matter of a law or ordinance.

_____6.   In *Plessy v Ferguson*, the United States Supreme Court ruled that the concept of "separate but equal" was an unconstitutional violation of the 14th Amendment.

_____7.   In *Mein Kampf*, Adolph Hitler designed his superior race concept around three groups of individuals: culture-bearing, culture-creating, and culture-destroying.

_____8.   In 1938, Emma Tenayuca staged an employee walkout at the Judson Candy Company in protest of the company's working conditions for pecan shellers.

_____9.   The Civil Rights Act of 1960 created the United States Commission of Civil Rights, and the Civil Rights Section of the United States Justice Department.

_____10.   In *Sweatt v Painter,* the United States Supreme Court ruled that the University of Texas's practice of denying African-American applicants to its own law school was constitutional since the Texas State University for Negroes had a program comparable to UT's Law School.

_____11.   Steering was the showing of properties to minorities located only in predominately minority residential areas.

_____12.   Native Americans did not gain citizenship until 1920 while voting rights were granted to them through a 1924 congressional law.

_____13.   In the 1960s, civil rights activist Cesar Chavez organized the United Canery Workers Union to bring attention to the working conditions of migrant farm workers.

_____14.   In *Near v Minnesota* (1931), the United States Supreme Court established the boundaries of "no prior restraint" for the print media.

_____15.   Civil rights encompass those unalienable rights that belong to individuals by the nature of humanity and which cannot be taken away without violating that humanity.

_____16.   In 2007, the Texas Legislature passed the Religious Viewpoints Anti-Discrimination Act requiring that public school districts adopt policies allowing for spontaneous religious expression by students.

_____17.   De jure discrimination is an undeliberate action that adversely impacts one group over another.

_____18.   In *Jim Crow America*, Earl Conrad develops the concept of economic racism.

_____19.   Native Americans were finally released from the control of the federal government with the passage of the Dawes Act in 1953.

_____20.   In *The Village of Skokie v the National Socialist Party* (1978), the United States Supreme Court ruled that the city of Skokie violated the right of assembly on the presumption of violence to the Nazi Party's wishes to stage a public march.

_____21.   Slander is verbal malicious attracts against another person.

_____22.   In *United States v Brian* (1968), the United States Supreme Court ruled that students wearing black arm bands in protest of the Vietnam War was a constitutional right to free speech.

_____23.   In *Everson v Board of Education of the Township of Ewing* (1947), the United States Supreme Court ruled that involuntary school-sponsored prayer was unconstitutional.

_____24.   In 1918, Annette Finnegan was the first woman to legally register to vote in Bexar County.

_____25.   The 13th Amendment to the United States Constitution guarantees due process and equal protection of the law to all citizens.

_____26.   Famed for writing *Uncle Tom's Cabin*, Harriet Beecher Stowe was a leading advocate against giving women voting rights.

_____27.   In 1972, women won an important battle with voters approved an Equal Rights Amendment to the Texas Constitution.

_____28.   Under Mexican rule, women in Texas had far more legal rights than women in the American colonies.

_____29   The United States Supreme Court has opted to the selective incorporation process to tie the amendments known as the Bill of Rights to the protections guaranteed to all in the 14 Amendment to the United States Constitution.

_____30.   The 1st Amendment to the Constitution guarantees the right of citizens to bear arms.

_____31.   The reading of biblical passages in a public school was ruled unconstitutional by the United States Supreme Court by its ruling in *Wallace v Jaffree*.

_____32.   According to the United States Supreme Court animal sacrifices as part of a religious ceremony are consitutionally protected under the 1st Amendment.

_____33.   The Mormon Church's practice of polygamy was outlawed by the United States Supreme Court's 1862 ruling in *Reynolds v United States*.

_____34.   The United States Supreme Court drew the line between acceptable and unacceptable speech with its ruling in *Schenck v United States* (1917).

_____35.   Congress and the White House have the constitutional backing "to stop the presses from rolling" on any news item or story they feel could be damaging to Congress or to the president.

_____36.   In *Brandenburg v Ohio*, the United States Supreme Court upheld a lower court's ruling that the actions of the local chapter of the KKK would present a clear and present danger and was therefore, illegal.

_____37.   In 1954, the federal government opted out of assimilation policies with Native Americans with the passage of the Indian Reorganization Act that urged a return to tribal identities.

_____38.   Redlining was the tactic of financial institutions denying loans to those who wanted to buy residential property in a racially changing neighborhood.

_____39.   An equal rights amendment to the Texas State Constitution was passed on March 30, 1972.

FILL-IN-THE-BLANK QUESTIONS: Write the appropriate word(s) to complete the sentence. The correct answers are given at the end of the study guides.

1. In _____ (1935), the United States Supreme Court eventually ruled that the protections offered in the Bill of Rights applied to all levels of government.

2. The courts have ruled that any speech that creates a _____ is unconstitutional.

3. The United States Constitution protects property rights with the _____ in Article I, Section. 10.

4. _____ are the acts of government intended to protect disadvantaged classes of persons or minority groups from arbitrary, unreasonable, or discriminatory treatment.

5. The _____ concept of racism is the belief that one group or culture is intellectually, genetically and culturally superior to any other group.

6. For Native Americans, the federal government has adopted a _____ formula, meaning that the degree of Native American blood a person claims determines their percentage of Native American heritage and subsequently, their rights to certain federal benefits.

7. The _____ of 1866 gave former slaves rights to property ownership as well as the rights to sue in court and make contractual agreements.

8. The National Association for the Advancement of Colored Persons was founded by_____ _____ in 1909.

9. Nationwide, women received the right to vote with the passage of the _____ to the United States Constitution.

10. As freedmen, many former slaves participated in the _____ system whereby they would work on someone else's farm in exchange for a modest wage, living accommodations and a small plot of land to grow their own vegetables.

11. The _____ of male superiority over women prevented women from securing the rights to hold a job, gain an education, vote, hold public office, etc.

12. _____ is an unfavorable action toward people because they are members of a particular racial or ethnic group.

13. The quest for women to gain the right to vote began in 1848 in Seneca Falls, New York, when_____ _____ delivered a speech entitled the *Declaration of Sentiments and Resolutions*.

14. _____ is collectively defined as the right of individuals and groups to be treated in humane ways and with respect for human dignity and personal well-being.

15. This phrase of the 1st Amendment "Congress shall make no laws respecting the establishment of religion" is called the _____.

16. _____ is the condition of being free from restrictions or constraints.

17. The concept of _____ is guided by the notion that the Anglo majority will gradually lose its economic and political clout to minority population groups.

18. African Americans were prohibited from moving into Anglo neighborhoods through the_____, a provision in a mortgage contract forbidding the future sale of the property to a minority.

19. In 1865, the United States Congress officially outlawed slavery with the passage of the _____ to the United States Constitution.

20. The concept of _____ rests on the belief that only those born on the soil of their native country should be the ones to benefit from that birthright.

21. _____ is as feeling or act of any individual or group in which a prejudgment about someone else or another group is made on the basis of emotion rather than on reason.

22. _____ refers to the manner in which a law, an ordinance, an administrative practice or judicial task is carried out.

23. _____ is the use of symbols, rather than words, to convey ideas.

24. Particularly in religious-based rulings, the United States Supreme Court has applied the _____, that is, federal funding for private, parochial and public schools is constitutional as long as its primary beneficiary is for the children who attend those schools.

25. Several prominent women in San Antonio formed the Equal Franchise Society of San Antonio and were known as the _____ since they held their meetings at the hotel.

26. In _____, the United States Supreme Court initially ruled that the United States Constitution's Bill of Rights applied only to the national government.

27. _____ of San Antonio founded the Women's Christian Temperance Union.

28. The "mother of the Texas Woman's Suffrage Movement" is _____, whose brother George founded a companion organization named the Men's League for Woman's Suffrage.

29. During the 85th Legislative Session, Governor Abbott signed into law Senate Bill 179 named after __ _____, a high school student who was a victim of intense cyberbullying that led to his suicide.

30. The first ten amendments to the United States Constitution are collectively known as the _____ _____.

31. _____ authorizes the Supreme Court to hold unconstitutional, and hence, unenforceable, any law or official action based upon a law, and any other action by a public official that it deems-upon careful reflection and in line with the inherent tradition of the law and judicial restraint-to be in conflict with the constitution.

32. In _____ (1961), the United States Supreme Court ruled unconstitutional a prayer written for all students to recite in the New Hyde Park School District as an unconstitutional violation of the 1st Amendment's guarantee of religious freedom.

33. _____ is speech without any conduct while fighting words are words that by their very nature inflict injury upon those to whom they are addressed.

34. In 1964, the United States Supreme Court ruled in _____, that an elected official whether it be the local police commissioner or the president of the United States is not constitutionally protected from fighting words since they are suspected targets of verbal and printed attacks.

35. The presidency of Richard Nixon took a near fatal blow when the United States Supreme Court ruled in _____ (1971) that the *New York Times* could legally printed excerpts of the *Pentagon Papers* detailing America's growing involvement in Vietnam.

36. The concept of _____ of the law and its application to our state and federal governments, is based on an extensive reservoir of constitutionally expressed and implied limitations upon governmental authority, and implied limitations upon governmental authority, ultimate determined by the judicial process.

37. _____ and others developed the underground railroad system that provided escape routes and safe houses and havens for fugitive slaves.

38. The United States Congress granted citizenship to former slaves with the passage of the _____ and voting rights to former male slaves with the passage of the _____to the United States Constitution.

39. Court-mandated public-school desegregation was launched by the United States Supreme Court's ruling in _____ (1954).

40. The settlement of the West was guided by _____, the desire to see the United States boundary from the Atlantic Ocean to the Pacific Ocean.

41. Collectively, clerical and secretarial jobs are called _____ jobs.

ESSAY QUESTIONS:

1. What is the separation of church and state doctrine? What religious rights are we guaranteed and what restrictions are placed upon those practices and beliefs?

2. What is the Patriot Act? Do you believe that the federal government has overstepped its boundaries in regards to the Bill of Rights? Provide specific examples.

3. What is the concept of "separate sisters"?

4. Although getting the right to vote was a major position for the American Suffrage organizations, what were some of the other social, political and economic interests expressed by members of the movement?

CHAPTER TWELVE – Social Service Public Policy Issues

CHAPTER SUMMARY: The rising number of people living in poverty is an on-going problem that continues to plague lawmakers in Washington, D.C., and Austin. This chapter examines the poverty-related and health care issues confronting Texans as well as discusses the policy options available to the state's lawmakers.

IDENTIFICATIONS: Briefly define the term or indicate the significance of the individual or the event.

Culture of Poverty

Disposal Income

Food Insecure

Department of Human Services

Model Cities

Per Capita Income

Survival of the Fittest

"Welfare Queens"

Homeless

TRUE/FALSE QUESTIONS: Indicate whether each statement is true (T) or false (F). The correct answers are given at the end of the study guides.

_____1.   The Bush administration did attempt a welfare reform package with the passage of the Personal Responsibility and Work Opportunity Reconciliation Act.

_____2.   The chronically homeless are individuals with a disability who have been continuously homeless for one year or more or have experienced at least four episodes of homelessness in the last three years where the combined length of time homeless in those occasions is at least twelve months.

_____3.   The temporarily or marginally poor are those whose incomes have fallen below the poverty level for over ten years.

_____4.   HUD estimates that 74 percent of extremely low-income renter households have a severe cost burden to even pay rent.

_____5.   Liberal perspectives hold that the undeserving poor are those who simply failed to avail themselves of the opportunities needed to improve their income situation.

_____6.   In the 1960s, President John Kennedy introduced a comprehensive approach to solving the nation's poverty-related problems called the War on Poverty Program.

_____7.   The Special Supplemental Program for Women, Infants and Children (WIC) is totally funded by the state of Texas to provide nutritional food staples to pregnant women.

_____8.   The Democratic Party embraced the liberal approach to poverty with the election of Harry Truman to the presidency.

_____9.   Over the past several years, national statistics indicate that the gap between the rich and poor is narrowing.

_____10.   The poverty level is basically calculated on the amount of money ranging from an individual to a family of nine spends on food.

_____11.   The working poor are those individuals whose annual incomes amount to less than half of the official poverty level.

_____12.   An individual is categorized as permanent or persistently poor if his/her income level has been below the poverty level for eight years or longer during a ten-year period.

_____13.   In Texas, adults lose their welfare benefits once their one to three year time limit has expired but their dependent children continue to receive benefits.

_____14.   The federal government draws a distinction between deserving and undeserving poor by placing as deserving of assistance the elderly, mentally ill, and the physically handicapped who through no fault of their own, have become impoverished.

_____15.   Federal law mandates that states participate in both the Medicaid and CHIP programs.

_____16.   In Texas, welfare recipients who are non-custodial parents will face loss of their driver's license and any professional certificates if they are delinquent in their child support payments.

_____17.   Nationwide, many seniors have purchased medigap insurance programs to provide coverage for medical costs not covered by Medicare.

_____18.   The Democratic Party follows the traditional conservative position that poverty is a self-inflicted result of one's individual failures and laziness to avail oneself of economic viability and mobility.

_____19.   The Personal Responsibility and Work Opportunity Act of 1996 places a ten-year lifetime limit of all benefits.

_____20. Relative poverty is determined by comparing an individual's income against society's overall standard of living.

_____21. As part of his New Deal package of relief, President Grover Cleveland created the Old Age Insurance program, a self-funded insurance plan providing pensions and benefits for the elderly and disabled.

_____22. Originally, Aid to Dependent Children (later changed to Aid to Families with Dependent Children) granted benefits only to women and her children, not to the traditional family unit of husband, wife and children.

_____23. Cash transfers provide direct payments to qualified recipients.

_____24. In-kind programs such as public housing, day care, Medicaid, WIC, Food Stamps, and, in some cases, legal services provide direct payments to the recipients of the benefits.

_____25. The federal food stamp program was launched in 1964 as part of President Kennedy's War on Poverty.

_____26. A household is declared as food insecure if members of that household were hungry at least some time during the period (usually a year) due to inadequate resources for food.

FILL-IN-THE-BLANK QUESTIONS: Write the appropriate word(s) to complete the sentence. The correct answers are given at the end of the study guides.

1. _____ is the minimum amount of income needed to survive without deprivation.

2. Several states pay their workers a _____, a rate above the federal minimum wage that is adjusted for increases in living costs.

3. The federal government provides potential homeowners with low incomes to apply for _____ housing subsidies as provided through the Housing and Community Development Act.

4. In the counties near the shared border with Mexico, many low-income Hispanics live in rural communities commonly known as the _____.

5. Since the American Revolution, the answer to indigent housing was the _____ commonly known as the poorhouse.

6. In _____, the United States Supreme Court ruled that Social Security is not an absolute guaranteed right.

7. The _____ of 1988 extended welfare benefits to qualifying two-parent families.

8. Developed in 1964, the _____ program provides an in-kind exchange of food coupons for food.

9. Created in 1965, the _____ program is a preventive health care system for low-income adults and their children.

10. In 1997, Congress enacted the _____, that provides free low-cost health insurance to the nation's uninsured children whose parents do not qualify for Medicaid but do not have the income to afford health insurance.

11. The _____ program provides cash payments to workers temporarily laid off from their jobs.

12. _____ is the nation's health care plan for the nation's senior citizens.

13. The modern welfare system was launched when the United States Congress passed the _____ in 1935.

14. The Medicare Prescription Drug Improvement and Modernization Act created a _____ gap in coverage.

15. _____ is the state of condition of being poor by lacking the means of providing material needs or comfort.

16. The _____ is a category of individuals with annual incomes amounting to less than half of the official poverty level.

17. A federally funded program, _____was designed to provide cash payments to low income elderly persons as well as to blind and disabled adults and children.

18. _____ is a household that has access at all times to enough food for an active healthy life for all household members, with no need for recourse to socially unacceptable food sources.

19. In 1999, the Texas Legislature replaced Aid to Families with Dependent Children (AFDC) with the _____.

20. _____ eligibility is based upon an applicant's demonstrated inability to provide for him/or herself the desired benefit due to the individual's depressed income level and assets.

21. _____ are benefits provided by government to which recipients have a legally enforceable right.

22. The eligibility level for numerous social service programs has a _____feature that provides services to those who incomes are slightly above the poverty level.

23. The _____ are those such as the elderly, the mentally, ill and the physically handicapped, who through no fault of their own became impoverished.

24. The _____ of poverty refers to the increased number of single-parent families headed by a woman whose income falls below the poverty level.

25. The _____ are typically undereducated high school dropouts either employed full time or part-time at minimum or below minimum wage salary levels.

26. HUD defines _____ as individual who are staying in emergency shelters, transitional housing or safe havens.

ESSAY QUESTIONS:

1. What was the settlement house? What services did it offer to the nation's poor and immigrant population groups?

2. In your opinion, what actions can the federal and state governments take to address poverty?

3. What measures should the federal government take to narrow the income gap between the nation's rich and poor?

CHAPTER THIRTEEN – Urban Governance and Public Policy Issues

CHAPTER SUMMARY: This chapter delves into the issues confronting today's mayors, city councils, and county governments are dealing with on a day-to-day basis. Like nationwide sister counterparts, Texas's cities are struggling to meet the increasing needs of their citizens against shrinking budgets.

IDENTIFICATION: Briefly define the term or indicate the significance of the individual or the event.

Cities As Partners In the Federal System

Contract for Deed

County or District Attorney

Frederick Law Olmstead

Fredericksburg

Galveston

Mina

Municipal Bonds

Recall Election

Term Limits

The German Belt

White Flight

Underclass

TRUE/FALSE QUESTIONS: Indicate whether each statement is true (T) or false (F). The correct answers are given at the end of the study guides.

_____1. Founded in 1824 by William Travis and Baron de Bastrop, the original name for Austin was San Felipe de Austin.

_____2. The United States Supreme Court ruled in *Dartmouth College v Woodward* (1819) that city dwellers could not on their own form a municipal government.

_____3. The lowest rung of judicial proceedings, district courts hear small claims civil suits and misdemeanor offenses.

_____4. An umbrella mortgage is a lending arrangement whereby the buyer is required to make a substantial down payment on the property with the understanding that the remaining balance is due as a lump sum when the loan matures.

_____5. Founded in 1718, San Antonio with its missions was the religious center of the Spanish/Mexican colonists.

_____6. The sheriff is the chief law enforcement officer for county government.

_____7. The federal government's initial program to provide communities with money to build affordable housing for middle- and low-income families occurred with the Section 8 Housing Bill of 1937.

_____8. Exclusionary zoning occurs when the original land developer or the original buyers in a suburb initiate restrictive covenants and building standards such as a mandated lot sizes and home square footage requirements.

_____9. Public goods are those products or services that can be individually packaged, sold or used.

_____10. Some county governments either appoint or elect a county treasurer with the primary duties of managing the county's money and issuing monthly financial reports.

_____11. One of the most cost efficient options of providing city services is to offer them based an individual's willingness and ability to pay for those services thereby denying those same services to those who simply cannot afford them.

_____12. The Department of Housing and Urban Development developed the Main Street Project to encourage city leaders to revamp their downtown areas.

_____13. Public goods are those items that can be used by all residents when needed.

_____14. A now outlawed discriminatory practice, a restrictive covenant actually was the practice of drawing a red line around deteriorating properties primarily in minority neighborhoods, marking them as a too high of a risk for predominately Anglos to qualify for a loan.

_____15. The county clerk's primary function is the serve as the county's keeper of all county-related legal documents.

_____16. Redlining is the division of a city into districts and the regulation of the types of buildings and activities permitted within districts.

_____17. White flight is the purposive efforts of city governments to bring back upper- and middle-income residents to their downtown areas by building high-rise condominiums.

_____18. An externality is an impact on a third party, one who is not directly involved as either the buyer or seller in a private transaction but who still either enjoys some benefit or suffers some negative consequence from the private exchange.

_____19. New Urbanism calls for the reconfiguration of sprawling suburbs into user-friendly neighborhoods with sidewalks, bike trails, inner-city parks, etc.

_____20. A new community center built with a combination of public and private sector money is an example of co-production.

_____21. Taking into account their future demographic changes, city and county governments can develop master plans that chart their community's development in five, ten or even twenty-year cycles.

_____22. Common pool goods are non-renewable goods such as water and oil that can be individually packaged, bartered and used, but their use by one person decreases the availability of that good for others.

_____23. The primary duties of the county sheriff are to manage both county and city jails and supervise all county law enforcement personnel.

_____24. A referendum election is usually held whenever city governments need citizen approval to initiate a tax for a proposed project.

_____25. In Spanish/Mexican Texas, it was the presidio that provided the colonists with protection from hostile Indian raids and the adverse conditions of frontier life.

_____26. Texas cities were granted extra territorial jurisdiction with the passage of the Municipal Annexation Act of 1963.

_____27. The Texas Legislature mandates that all counties with a population of over 10,000 must have a county auditor who is appointed by the district court judge or judges having jurisdiction in the county.

FILL-IN-THE-BLANK QUESTIONS: Write the appropriate word(s) to complete the sentence. The correct answers are given at the end of the study guides.

1. Fearful of future deterioration of their neighborhoods, many residents are forming their own _____ to enforce proper maintenance of their properties.

2. Incorporate cities within a major metropolitan area commonly known as _____.

3. According to the Texas Constitution, there are four basic units of local government in Texas: municipal or city, independent school districts, _____,and _____ _____.

4. In the _____ arrangement the mayor is elected in a city-wide or at-large election with council members elected from either single- or a combination of single- and multi-member districts.

5. A county's official record keeper of vital records is the _____.

6. Other states have opted for a_____ plan whereby the duplicated services provided by both city and county governments are merged into one governing authority.

7. Counties are governed by a _____ consisting of a county judge and four commissioners.

8. Cities such as San Antonio use the _____ format whereby the city council establishes policy and procedures for the city and the city manager is responsible for the day-to-day administration of the city.

9. An _____ is an official document ordering the city council to mandate an election for the citizens to approve a change in policy or a new service.

10. _____cities are basically governed by the Texas Legislature.

11. A _____ is a unit of local government typically performing a single function and overlapping traditional political boundaries.

12. The duties of the _____includes collecting tax obligations for his/her county government as well as issuing certificates of title and collecting license fees for motor vehicles.

13. In the _____ format, the mayor serves as both the executive and administrative head of city government.

14. Self-governing through a city charter, _____have the authority to pass ordinances.

15. _____ is the addition by a city of land adjunct to it as an aggressive policy of growth or to meet the problems of metropolitan expansion.

16. The _____ of a city is the pursuit of economic viability.

17. Commonly known as the _____, an 1868 Iowa court ruling upheld Dartmouth by clearly stating that municipal governments owe their origin, their powers, and their ultimate survival to their state legislative houses.

18. An _____ is a local decree that has the force of the law.

19. Rarely used, the _____ format of city government operates without a mayor since the legislative and administrative powers are divided among several elected commissioners.

20. The "downtown" area of a city is commonly known as the _____.

21. In the _____ format, the mayor has no real direct governing authority over city council members or city staff.

22. The _____ specifies the powers and duties of elected city leadership to include candidate qualifications, terms of office, types of services, etc.

23. The _____ passed in 1913 essentially divided Texas's cities into two groups – home rule and general law cities.

24. A city's _____ extends from 0.5 to 1.5 miles on all sides beyond their current city boundary lines.

25. The _____ side of a city is the development of policies focusing on quality-of-life issues for city residents.

26. Suburban areas can avoid annexation by petitioning for _____ to become a self-governing city.

27. The _____ format actually strips the mayor of any independent governing authority and considers this position to be on the same level as the city council members.

28. Water and oil are _____ common pool goods that can be individually packaged, bartered and used, but their use by one person decreases the availability of these goods for others.

29. Competition among cities to land a major new business involves city leaders granting a lucrative _____ _____ plan to seal the deal.

30. _____ is the division of a city into districts and the regulation of the types of buildings and activities permitted within each district.

ESSAY QUESTIONS:

1. Why did the frontier-style gradually give way to an urban life style?

2. What are the pluses and minuses to term limits in city government?

3. What are the primary functions of county governments in Texas?

4. In your opinion, is exclusionary zoning a form of housing discrimination? Support your response.

CHAPTER FOURTEEN – The Politics of Highways and Transportation

CHAPTER SUMMARY: Frontier life in Texas was hampered by the state's dismal transportation system. The Camino Real or the King's Highway was just a path. Today, Texas has an extensive but very expensive highway system that fits the automobile mentality. This chapter discusses the development of the state's transportation system and delves into the complexities of maintaining the current system while at the same time meeting the ever changing transportation needs of Texans.

IDENTIFICATIONS: Briefly define the term or indicate the significance of the individual or the event.

Americans with Disabilities Act (ADA)

DART

Dedicated Funds

Engineer-Director (Department of Transportation Commission)

Federal Highway Administration

Highway 281

Light Rail

Motor Fuels Tax

Park and Ride

The Anti-Highway Lobby

Good Bridge

Surface Transportation Assistance Act

TRUE/FALSE QUESTIONS: Indicate whether each statement is true (T) or false (F). The correct answers are given at the end of the study guides.

_____1. The Transportation Equity Act increased the federal gasoline tax from five to nine cents per gallon with four cents earmarked for the repair, maintenance, and construction of interstate highway systems.

_____2. The Urban Mass Transportation Act provided federal funding for the construction and operation of mass transportation systems.

_____3. In Texas, the lion's share of the state budget's is spent on public or mass transportation while only a small proportion of the budget is allocated to highway or private transportation projects.

_____4. Intrastate commerce is controlled by the federal government while interstate commerce is overseen by state governments.

_____5. Railroads appeared in Texas as early as 1836 as the newly formed Republic sponsored the ill-fated Texas Railroad Navigation and Banking Center.

_____6. The first mandated automobile speed limit in Texas was established in 1907 at twenty-miles-per-hour.

_____7. With the passage of NAFTA, border states pushed for the federal government to provide additional money to upgrade the interstate highways passing through their states.

_____8. The Texas Legislature has passed several highway safety measures to include canvas covers on dump trucks, mandatory seat belt laws and a law prohibiting children from riding in the bed of a pickup truck.

_____9. The primary costs of the state's highway system is for maintenance of existing highways and construction and land acquisition for new highways, making it the largest budgetary expense in the state's budget.

_____10. The dedicated budget account to fund the state's roadway systems was the brainstorm of Price Daniel, the state's pro-highway governor.

_____11. The state's road and expressway systems are funded through a series of progressive tax programs to include the motor fuels tax, automobile registration fees, road user fees, etc.

_____12. In the Texas Legislature, Republicans favor a move towards mass transportation systems while Democrats support the private automobile-highway mentality.

_____13. It is estimated that 75 percent of the state's roads remain the responsibility of county and city governments.

_____14. During the 1970s, the federal government mandated that states lower their speed limits to 45 mph on all major roads to include highways as a way to conserve energy.

_____15. The Highway Act of 1944 solidified the federal government's commitment to build a nationwide interstate highway system.

_____16. Automobiles first appeared in Texas about the early 1900s.

_____17. Initially, roads were the sole responsibility of the federal government with little or no role for state or local governing units.

_____18. The Texas Department of Transportation Commission is composed of six-members elected by the public for six-year overlapping terms.

_____19. Recently, the United States Congress lifted its mandated federal speed limits opting instead for state legislative houses to set their own limits.

_____20. Currently, the United States Secretary of Transportation is responsible for the United States Coast Guard, the Federal Aviation Agency, Federal Highway Administration, National Highway Safety Bureau, Federal Railroad Administration, Urban mass Transportation Administration, and the St. Lawrence Seaway Development Corporation.

_____21. By 1840, the Buffalo Bayou near Houston was abandoned due to lack of funding.

_____22. The American Recovery and Reinvestment Act provided billions to states for the development of mass transportation systems.

_____23. The National Minimum Drinking Age Act lowered the legal drinking age from twenty-one to eighteen.

_____24. Both the Federal Aid Highway Act and the Highway Revenue Act mandated a four-cent-per-gallon gasoline tax to fund the newly created Federal Highway Trust Fund.

_____25. The National Industrial Recovery Act under the Truman Administration allocated at least one-fourth of the federal-aid highway funds for extensions of roads through incorporated municipalities.

_____26. The Bureau of Public Roads was created by the federal government to ensure that individual state roadways connected to each other at their share boundary lines.

_____27. As part of his New Deal plan, Theodore Roosevelt used the Works Progress Administration to put unemployed Americans to work fixing the nation's transportation system.

_____28. The federal government demonstrated its intentions to build a nationwide federal highway system with the passage of the Federal Road Act in 1916.

_____29. The federal government showed its support for mass transportation systems with the passage in 1982 of the Surface Transportation Assistance Act.

FILL-IN-THE-BLANK QUESTIONS: Write the appropriate word(s) to complete the sentence. The correct answers are given at the end of the study guides.

1. In 1857, the San Antonio-San Diego Mail route was established with Aug's Settlement Inn at Leon Springs being the first stop of the _____.

2. To combat the illegal practices of the Texas Traffic Association, _____created the Texas Railroad Commission to regulate the state's railroads.

3. In 1966, the United States Congress created the _____a cabinet-level position to oversee the nation's transportation systems.

4. The leading supporter of highways in Texas is the powerful _____founded in 1911.

5. A _____ is a road or highway lane reserved exclusively for buses.

6. The _____ (1963) provided federal money to those metropolitan areas promoting both private highway systems and public transportation programs.

7. _____ are small vans that provide group personalized door-to-door services.

8. In 1991, a bullet train was blocked by the _____, a lobbying group funded in part by Southwest Airlines.

9. Angry over the abusive practices of the railroads, delegates to the 1876 Constitutional Convention issued to battle cry to _____.

10. Approximately 70 percent of the state's traffic falls under the supervision of the _____ commonly known as TxDOT.

11. The primary task of the federal government's _____ is to ensure that individual state roadways are connected to each other at their shared boundary lines.

12. Mini-buses or _____ provide shuttle services between hotels and convention centers.

13. The Federal Highway Administration defines a _____as one that is dilapidated or overburdened for their current traffic.

14. The _____ passed during the Johnson administration places stiff guidelines on the use of highway signage.

15. Running from San Juan Bautisa on the Rio Grande to Bexar, the Camino Real was also known as the ___ _____.

16. The _____ of Article I of the United States Constitution gives the federal government the authority to oversee interstate commerce.

17. A depression-era program, the _____ put millions of Americans back to work either repair existing roads or building new highways across the nation.

18. Toll roads are _____ roadways whereby travelers pay to use them.

19. A _____ is a lane on a street or a highway that is reserved for buses and vehicles with at least two to three passengers.

20. To warn motorists of dangerous road conditions and traffic accidents, TxDOT has installed an overhead computer-generated warning system commonly known as _____.

21. The state's Highway Fund is an example of a _____.

22. The _____ Act provided emergency loans for commuter railroads and modest cash outlays for pilot master transportation projects.

23. Now known as the Department of Transportation Commission, the Texas _____ ____ _____was created in 1917.

24. The _____ is composed of all transportation-oriented business and interest groups.

25. In 1876, the Texas Legislature passed a _____, allocating sixteen sections of land to railroad companies for every mile of track they completed.

ESSAY QUESTIONS:

1. Who are the primary members of the Texas Highway Lobby? Specifically what does each group gain with the building of new highways?

2. In your opinion, is the state's mass transportation system user friendly to all groups such as the elderly and handicapped? Support your response.

3. What are the problems associated with traffic snarls?

CHAPTER FIFTEEN – Education Policy in Texas

CHAPTER SUMMARY: The chapter examines the historical development of the Texas public and higher education institutions with a detailed analysis of the current curriculum issues and budget concerns confronting the state's education system.

IDENTIFICATIONS: Briefly define the term or indicate the significance of the individual or the event.

Board of Regents

Board of Trustees

Community College

Educational Consolidation and Improvement Act

Edgewood v Kirby

Higher Education Assistance Fund

Hopwood v Texas

Permanent University Fund

Santa Rita Well

Southern Association of Colleges and Schools

Texas Higher Education Coordinating Board

Voucher System

Morrill Act (1862)

TRUE/FALSE QUESTIONS: Indicate whether each statement is true (T) or false (F). The correct answers are given at the end of the study guides.

_____1. Title I of the Elementary and Secondary Education Act provides federal funds for the purchase of library books and instructional materials.

_____2. According to the 1983 *Nation at Risk* study, approximately 13 percent of the nation's seventeen-year-olds were functionally illiterate.

_____3. Under No Child Left Behind, all schools were required to develop periodic report cards showing parents their child's standardized test scores.

_____4. The Texas Constitution of 1876 called for public funding and land grants for the establishment of both private and public schools.

_____5. Although E. J. Davis believed in centralization of government functions, he mandated that the state's education system must be manned at the local level.

_____6. By 1915, the Texas Legislature required that all children between ages six and eighteen be enrolled and attend a public school for at least 150 days per year.

_____7. Under the Gilmer-Aiken reforms, all applicants for a teaching position in a public school had to have a valid Texas teacher's certificate.

_____8. Along with severe budget cuts, the 2011 Texas Legislature mandated that all classroom sizes regardless of grade level be increased to 24 or 25 students.

_____9. The State Board of Education is composed of fifteen members appointed by the governor for four-year staggered terms of office.

_____10. Traditionally, public school board members have the tendency to overly micromanage and meddle into the day-to-day operations of the schools.

_____11. The state's first public college in Texas was Texas Agricultural and Mechanical College, now known as Texas A & M opened its doors in 1876.

_____12. Chaired by Ross Perot, the SCOPE committee recommended increasing the maximum class sizes and raising the passing grade for courses from 60 to 70.

_____13. The University of Texas launched its academic programs in 1883.

_____14. The Texas Constitution of 1845 officially mandated the establishment of a system of schools and officially pledged that one/tenth of the state's annual revenue from taxation would be set aside for education.

_____15. The Smith Hughes Act passed in 1862 provided land grants for the establishment of college-level agricultural and mechanical arts programs.

_____16. Under No Child Left Behind, a stage one sanction would require that the entire school staff would be replaced, the school day would be extended, and the principal would be stripped of his/her authority.

_____17. The SCOPE Committee's recommendations coupled with HB 72 proved to be so popular with Texans that Mark White easily won re-election to the governorship.

_____18. The conservative approach to public schools in Texas mirror the philosophy of John Stuart Mill who stressed that man's creativity must be encouraged, not suppressed.

_____19. Appointed by the governor with Senate confirmation, the Commissioner of Education is selected from the members of the board for a two-year term.

_____20. Under HB 72, all of the state's teachers were required to take a basic literacy test with the possibility of losing their teaching credentials if they failed the test.

_____21. A constitutional amendment approved in 1918 mandates that the state issue free textbooks to all students enrolled in public schools.

_____22. The Texas Constitution of 1876 returned control of the state's public schools to local communities.

_____23. A 2003 congressional law mandated that all of the nation's public schools must declare that prayer is not allowed in or outside of the classrooms.

_____24. A provision of the Civil Rights Act of 1964 enabled the federal government to punish schools for non-compliance particularly for discriminatory practices.

_____25. Both the National Science Foundation and the National Endowment for the Arts and Humanities were created by the United States Congress to encourage scientific research and academic programs in the arts and humanities.

FILL-IN-THE-BLANK QUESTIONS: Write the appropriate word(s) to complete the sentence. The correct answers are given at the end of the study guides.

1. The _____ (1917) provided federal grants for vocational college programs.

2. The _____ (1972) eliminated minority group segregation and discriminatory practices in elementary and secondary schools.

3. Once in the White House, President George W. Bush initiated his package of public school reform measures under the umbrella of the _____Program.

4. Initially, _____ in Texas were one building schools located in rural areas while independent schools were located in urban areas.

5. The state's major education reform package happened in 1949 with the passage of the _____.

6. The most controversial part of HB 72 was the _____ provision that adversely impacted public school athletic and band programs.

7. Created in 1949, the _____ oversees the Texas Education Agency.

8. In 1991, Governor Ann Richards was instrumental in convincing the Texas Legislature to mandate that all students take and pass a series of tests known as the _____,

9. A _____is a student who is enrolled in public schools in Grades 7-12, does not return to finish school the following fall, is not expelled, and does not graduate or receive a GED.

10. _____ is the funds a public school system has above the state-mandated per-pupil expenditure.

11. In the landmark United States Supreme Court case _____, the court of last resort ruled that although the public school funding system in Texas is unfair to the state's property poor schools district, the funding formula is not unconstitutional.

12. The process of selecting textbooks for the public schools in Texas falls upon the shoulders of the _____.

13. _____are governed by county-wide elected superintendents and trustees.

14. In 1972 the federal government established federal grant assistance to college students under a program commonly known as the _____.

15. The initial entry of the federal government into the nation's education system was the passage of the _____ of 1785 which provided one section of land in each township for the endowment of schools.

16. Texas has initiated a limited _____whereby parents can use them to pay the tuition and transportation costs to send their children to the schools of their choice.

17. In Texas, all property appraisals are based on _____,meaning the fair market value of the property.

18. Public school are assessed on their, _____,defined as the percentage of students from a class of beginning seventh or ninth graders who graduate, receive a GED, or are still enrolled in the fall after graduation.

19. According to the Texas Education Agency, an _____ student is one that is eligible for free or reduced-priced meals under the National School Lunch and Children Nutrition Program.

20. _____ are directly supervised by elected board members under the guidance of the Texas Education Agency.

21. In 1982, Governor Mark White announced the formation of the _____ or SCOPE to develop a reform package for the state's public school systems.

22. President Obama's series of education reform efforts were incorporated under the _____ _____ which pledge a quality educational opportunity from cradle through career.

23. In 1983, the nation's education system was in a frenzy when the national Commission on Excellence in Education issued its study titled _____which revealed the nationwide serious problems within the public school system.

24. A former classroom teacher, _____ was the primary catalyst behind the passage of the Elementary and Secondary Education Act of 1965.

25. The Servicemen's Readjustment Act (1944) is commonly known as the _____.

26. In 1944, the United States Congress passed the _____ designed to provide World War II veterans with financial education assistance.

27. The _____ is the primary agency overseen by its policy-making body the State Board of Education.

28. To equal funding inequities between property rich and property poor school districts, the Texas Legislative invented the _____ plan whereby property rich school districts would 'give up' some of their state money to equal state funding for property poor districts.

ESSAY QUESTIONS:

1. What was the impact of the Gilmer-Akin reforms on public education?

2. What was the impact of the No Child Left Behind reform package on public education?

3. What was the impact of Ross Perot's SCOPE committee recommendations on the state's public school system?

CHAPTER SIXTEEN – Texans and Their Environment

CHAPTER SUMMARY: This chapter examines the issues confronting Texans over the quality of its environment and the steps taken to protect it from future damage. In addition, the chapter delves into the confrontational battleground between property-rights and land ownership over legislative mandates regarding environmental issues.

IDENTIFICATION: Briefly define the term or indicate the significance of the individual or the event.

Atomic Energy Act (1954)

Corps of Engineers

Edwards Aquifer

John Muir

George Perkins Marsh

Koyto Agreement

Lady Bird Johnson

Maquiladoras

Silent Spring

Yellowstone National Park

Paris Climate Agreement

Clean Air Act (1963)

Wilderness Act (1964)

Endangered Species Act (1973)

Ozone

Municipal Solid Waste

Health and Human Services Commission

TRUE/FALSE QUESTIONS: Indicate whether each statement is true (T) or false (F). The correct answers are given at the end of the study guides.

_____1. Woodrow Wilson was instrumental in securing passage of legislation creating the United States Forestry Service.

_____2. President Barack Obama's environmental issues included the promotion of alternative energy sources to gradually eliminate the nation's dependency upon fossil fuels.

_____3. According the rule of capture, all percolating groundwater such as a spring belongs to the owners of the land where it was found.

_____4. The Texas Department of Agriculture enforces all state laws concerning game, fish, oysters and marine life, and manages recreational and historical sites.

_____5. The Padre National Wildlife Refuge was created in 1937 when the federal government purchased over 54,000 acres of Texas coastline for conservation purposes.

_____6. According to the Endangered Species Act, an endangered species is one that is likely to become endangered in the foreseeable future.

_____7. President Bill Clinton used the General Revision Act to place millions of acres of land under federal protection.

_____8. Passed in 1900, the Lacey Act bans hunting in all national parks.

_____9. A 1944 treaty signed between the United States and Mexico mandates that both nations share water in the reservoirs on the Rio Grande River.

_____10. The Pittman-Robertson Act establishes strict standards to protect workers from on-the-job exposure to hazardous chemicals, materials, and so forth.

_____11. The Texas Hazardous Substance Spill Prevention and Control Act establishes regulations for the notification and cleanup of spills and discharges of hazardous substances in the state's waters.

_____12. Acid rain is wide-scale, low-level pollution that obstructs visibility.

_____13. A waterway declared impaired cannot support aquatic life and is unsafe for fishing and swimming.

_____14. The 1899 Refuse Act mandated that any business seeking to dump waste to navigable rivers had to first obtain a permit from the Corps of Engineers.

_____15. A waterway can be rated as threatened, meaning that if the pollution levels are not reduced to acceptable standards, the body of water is uninhabitable for plans, wildlife, marine life, and people.

_____16. If a city or state's air quality is declared as non-compliant, the Environmental Protection Agency is empowered to assess daily fines until attainment or compliance has been achieved.

_____17. The Safe Drinking Water Act of 1972 establishes the framework for overseeing water pollution standards across the nation.

_____18. The Environmental Protection Agency has regulatory control over hazardous wastes, noise pollution, pesticides and endangered species.

_____19. On the average, Republican presidents have been supportive of the EPA and allows the agency to take a more aggressive role against polluters by supporting stronger regulations and increases to the EPA's budget.

_____20. The Clean Water Act also known as the Safe Drinking Water Act, establishes federal standards to ensure that water suppliers servicing more than twenty-five people provide safe water for human consumption.

_____21. Acid rain is a complex chemical and atmospheric phenomenon that occurs when emissions of sulfur and nitrogen compounds and other substances are transformed by chemical processes in the atmosphere, often far from the original source, and then deposited on earth in either wet or dry form.

_____22. The Texas Department of Parks and Wildlife plays a role in the regulation of offshore oil exploration and well as protection of sand dunes, coastal areas and wetlands.

_____23. The National Pollution Discharge Elimination System (NPDES) requires all businesses and industries to file a permit to discharge the dumping of any effluents into a waterway.

_____24. President George W. Bush's pro-environmental positions clearly placed him at odds with his fellow Republicans who wanted less environmental regulations.

_____25. Big Bend National Park has been recently listed by the Environmental Protection Agency as an endangered parkland.

_____26. A threatened species is one likely to become endangered in the foreseeable future.

FILL-IN-THE-BLANK QUESTIONS: Write the appropriate word(s) to complete the sentence. The correct answers are given at the end of the study guides.

1. The Environmental Protection Agency has established _____NAAQS for acceptable levels of carbon monoxide, sulfur dioxide, ozone, lead, nitrogen dioxide and particulate matter.

2. _____is human additions of undesirable substances into the environment.

3. _____ is groundwater, percolating or otherwise, lakes, bays, ponds, impounding reservoirs, springs, rivers, streams, creeks, estuaries, wetlands, marshes, inlets, canals, the Gulf of Mexico and all other bodies of surface water.

4. According to the Texas Water Code, the _____is that portion of a belt of porous, water-bearing limestone composed of the Comanche Peak, Edwards and Georgetown formations trending from west to east to northeast through Kinney, Uvalde, Medina, Bexar, Kendall, Comal and Hays counties.

5. _____ is defined as a group of chemical compounds that are in the wrong place or in the wrong concentration at the wrong time.

6. _____ refers to a family of inert, non-toxic and easily-liquefied chemicals used in refrigeration, air conditioning, packaging, and insulation or as solvents or aerosol propellants.

7. _____ is defined as any garbage, rubbish, sludge from a waste treatment plant, water supply, treatment plant or air pollution control facility, and other discarded materials.

8. The Comprehensive Environmental Response, Compensation and Liability Act created the federal government's _____ to clean up toxic waste dumps.

9. _____ is an area where the earth and its community of life are untrammeled by man, where man himself is a visitor who does not remain.

10. _____ is solid waste resulting from or incidental to municipal, community, commercial, institutional, and recreational activities including garbage, rubbish, ashes, street cleanings, dead animals, abandoned automobiles, and all other solid waste other than industrial waste.

11. _____ include ash, smoke, dust, soot, and liquid droplets released through the burning of fuels and the use of pesticides.

12. _____ are defined as areas that are inundated or saturated by surface or groundwater at a frequency and duration sufficient to support, and that under normal circumstances do support, a prevalence of vegetation typically adapted for life in saturated soil conditions.

13. An _____ is a coastal area where fresh water from rivers and streams comes together with the salt water from the ocean.

14. _____ pollution is a pollution source that has a precise, identifiable location such as a pipe or a smokestack.

15. In 1892, John Muir founded the _____, now hailed as one of the nation's most prestigious environmental groups.

16. _____ is the alternation of the physical, thermal, chemical or biological quality injurious to humans, animal life, vegetation or property or to public health, safety or welfare, or impairs the usefulness or the public enjoyment of the water for any lawful or reasonable purpose.

17. A _____ is the coastal waters and the adjacent shorelines, strongly influenced by each other in proximity to the shorelines of the several coastal states to include islands, transitional and intertidal area, salt marshes, wetlands and beaches.

18. _____ occurs when nitrogen oxides produced by burning fuel and volatile organic compounds escape into the atmosphere.

19. _____ is a mixture of nitrogen, oxygen, argon, carbon dioxide along with traces of neon, helium, krypton, hydrogen, xenon, methane, and vitreous dioxide.

20. An _____ of water is approximately 325,851 gallons.

21. _____ is water distributed by an individual or public or private agency for human consumption.

22. _____ is sewage, industrial waste, municipal waste, recreational waste, agricultural waste or other waste.

23. _____ pollution is diffused with no clear indication as to its origination.

24. By federal law, all federal agencies are required to submit an _____ for every federal project that indicates the existing harm the project will pose to the environment and the steps to be taken to avoid an adverse impact.

25. _____ was the nation's first wildlife sanctuary.

26. If a business, industrial complex, etc., meets its national ambient air quality standards, it is rated as attainment, however, a business, industrial complex, etc., can be declared as _____ if they do not meet those standards and are now subjected to costly daily fines until attainment is reached.

27. The _____ (1974) sets acceptable standards for the quality of drinking water for suppliers serving more than twenty-five people.

28. The _____ is the amount of oxygen required for decomposition of a given amount of waste.

ESSAY QUESTIONS:

1. What are some of the complaints against the Environmental Protection Agency?

2. Why did the voters of San Antonio turn down the Applewhite water project?

3. What was and is Mitchell Lake?

STUDY GUIDE ANSWERS

CHAPTER ONE – A Brief Historical and Culture Overview of Texas

True/False Questions:

1. True
2. True
3. False
4. True
5. True
6. True
7. True
8. True
9. True
10. True
11. False
12. True
13. True
14. False
15. False
16. True
17. False
18. False
19. True
20. True
21. False
22. False
23. True
24. False
25. False
26. True
27. True
28. False
29. True

Fill-in-the-Blank Questions:

1. Payayas
2. Treaty of Velasco
3. Twin Sisters
4. Col. Juan Seguin
5. Terry's Texas Rangers
6. San Patricio; Refugio
7. Jim Crow Laws
8. Stephen F. Austin
9. James Hogg
10. Green De Witt
11. John Tower
12. Terrell Election Law
13. John Tyler
14. Runaway Scrape
15. Ricon de Santa Gertrudis
16. Mestizo; Tejano
17. Alonzo Alverez de Penida
18. Scorched Earth
19. Cat Spring; Panna Maria
20. Mission San Antonio de Valero
21. Benjamin Edwards
22. Senora Francisca Alverez
23. Alsatians
24. Henry Smith
25. Canary Islands
26. Augustus Magee
27. Sam Houston, Maribeau Lamar
28. Law of April 6, 1830
29. Goodnight-Loving

CHAPTER TWO– Interest Groups

True/False Questions:

1. False
2. True
3. True
4. False
5. False

Fill-in-the-Blank Questions:

1. Advocacy Groups
2. Pluralism
3. Samuel Gompers
4. Political Action Committees
5. Lobbyist

6. True		6.	Bribery
7. False		7.	Peak Association
8. False		8.	Texas Ethics Commission
9. True		9.	W.E.B. Dubois
10. True		10.	Interest Aggregation
11. False		11.	Collective Bargaining
12. False		12.	Access
13. False		13.	Gridlock
14. True		14.	Tea Pot Dome
15. False		15.	Selective Benefits
16. True		16.	Elitism
17. True		17.	Free Rider
18. True		18.	Indirect Lobbying
19. True		19.	Daughters of the Republic of Texas
20. True		20.	American Public Works Association
21. False		21.	Interest Group Liberalism
22. False		22.	League of United Latin American Citizens
23. True		23.	The Grange
24. True		24.	National Civic League
25. True		25.	Hyperpluralism
26. False		26.	The Establishment
27. True		27.	Pressure Group
28. False		28.	*Moore v Dempsey*
29. True		29.	Taft-Hartley Act

CHAPTER THREE – Political Parties

True/False Questions:

Fill-in-the-Blank Questions:

1. False		1.	Loyal Opposition
2. True		2.	Platform
3. True		3.	Party Organization
4. False		4.	Conservatism
5. True		5.	Liberalism
6. False		6.	Boll Weevils
7. False		7.	Woodrow Wilson
8. False		8.	Know-Nothing Party
9. True		9.	La Raza Unida Party
10. False		10.	Populist Party
11. True		11.	Ramsey Muniz
12. False		12.	Ideology
13. False		13.	Iron Law of Oligarchy
14. True		14.	Faction
15. False		15.	Political Party
16. True		16.	Texas Two-Step
17. True		17.	Cultural Conservatism

18. False
19. True
20. True
21. True
22. False
23. False
24. True
25. False
26. False
27. False

18. Centrist
19. Individualism
20. Third Party
21. Greenbacks
22. Theodore Roosevelt
23. *Cousins v Wigoda*
24. Consensual Party System
25. Federalist Party/Jefferson Republicans
26. *Democratic Party v LaFollette*
27. Libertarians

CHAPTER FOUR – Elections – Texas Style

True/False Questions:

1. True
2. True
3. False
4. True
5. False
6. True
7. False
8. False
9. True
10. False
11. False
12. False
13. False
14. False
15. False
16. False
17. True
18. False
19. False
20. True
21. False
22. True
23. True
24. True
25. False
26. False
27. True
28. False
29. True
30. False
31. True

Fill-in-the-Blank Questions:

1. Participatory Democracy
2. Direct Primary
3. Blanket Primary
4. Crossover
5. Poll
6. *Oregon v Mitchell*
7. Coattail Effect
8. Political Culture
9. Political Efficacy
10. Evaluative Orientations
11. Thirty Days
12. Political Socialization Process
13. Winner-Take-All
14. Office Block
15. Pappy O'Daniel
16. Terrell Elections Law
17. Critical Election
18. Australian Ballot
19. Hard Money
20. Revenue Act
21. Help America Vote Act
22. Deviating Election
23. Special Election
24. Primary Election
25. John Locke
26. *Harper v Virginia State Board of Education*

CHAPTER FIVE – Intergovernmental Relationships

True/False Questions:

1. True
2. False
3. False
4. True
5. True
6. True
7. True
8. False
9. True
10. True
11. True
12. True
13. False
14. True
15. False
16. True
17. False
18. True
19. True
20. False
21. False
22. True
23. False
24. False
25. False
26. False
27. True
28. False
29. False
30. True
31. False
32. False

Fill-in-the-Blank Questions:

1. Unitary System
2. Vertical Federalism
3. Judiciary Act
4. *Texas v White*
5. Pragmatic Federalism
6. Unfunded Mandate
7. John Jay
8. Eminent Domain
9. Compact Theory
10. Lyndon Johnson
11. Grants-in-Aid
12. Dual Federalism
13. *United States v Lopez*
14. Horizontal Federalism
15. Confederation
16. Implied Powers
17. Robin Hood Approach
18. No Child Left Behind
19. Patriot Act
20. Interstate Compact
21. Direct Order
22. Interposition
23. 10th
24. Enumerated Powers
25. Federalism
26. Article I
27. 10
28. *Gibbons v Ogden*
29. *South Carolina v Baker*
30. Concurrent Majority
31. New Federalism
32. Mandates

CHAPTER SIX – The Texas Constitution

True/False Questions:

1. False
2. True
3. True
4. True
5. True

Fill-in-the-Blank Questions:

1. Constitutionalism
2. Government
3. Promulgation
4. Homestead Provision
5. Thomas Paine

6. False		6.	James Madison
7. False		7.	Preamble
8. True		8.	Unitary
9. False		9.	A. J. Hamilton
10. True		10.	Social Contract
11. True		11.	Obnoxious Act
12. False		12.	Decree
13. True		13.	Representative Democracy
14. False		14.	Constitution
15. True		15.	Magna Carta
16. True		16.	Ideology
17. False		17.	Charles de Montesquieu
18. True		18.	Checks and Balances/Separation of Powers
19. True		19.	Retrenchment and Reform
20. False		20.	Bifurcated
21. True		21.	Jose Antonio Navarro
22. True			
23. False			
24. True			
25. True			

CHAPTER SEVEN – The Legislative Branch of Texas

True/False Questions:

Fill-in-the-Blank Questions:

1. False	1.	Dennis Bonnen
2. True	2.	*Shelby County v Holder*
3. True	3.	Special Bill
4. False	4.	Resolutions
5. False	5.	Local
6. False	6.	Filibuster
7. False	7.	Cloture
8. False	8.	Recess Appointment
9. False	9.	Major State
10. True	10.	Ad Hoc Committees
11. False	11.	Simple Resolution
12. False	12.	Apportionment
13. True	13.	Resolutions
14. False	14.	Redistricting
15. False	15.	*Kilgarlin v Martin*
16. True	16.	Pork Barrel Legislation
17. True	17.	Discharge Petition
18. True	18.	Joint Session
19. True	19.	*League of United American Citizens v Perry*
20. True	20.	Impeachment
21. False	21.	*Thornburg v Gingles*

22. True	22.	Legislative Audit Committee
23. False	23.	Rules and Resolutions Committee
24. True	24.	Ghost voting
25. False	25.	150/31
26. True	26.	*Wesberry v Sanders*

CHAPTER EIGHT – The Executive Branch of Texas Government

True/False Questions: Fill-in-the-Blank Questions:

1. False	1.	Dolph Briscoe
2. True	2.	John Connally
3. False	3.	Post-Adjournment Veto
4. True	4.	Jim Ferguson
5. True	5.	Coke Stevenson
6. False	6.	Secretary of State
7. True	7.	Bill Hobby
8. True	8.	Carole Keeton Strayhorn
9. False	9.	Bureaucracy
10. False	10.	Texas Railroad Commission
11. True	11.	Iron Triangle
12. False	12.	Recess Appointment
13. True	13.	Mirabeau B. Lamar
14. True	14.	Ann Richards
15. True	15.	Plural Executive
16. False	16.	Father's Day Massacre
17. False	17.	Attorney General
18. False	18.	Quasi-legislative/Quasi-judicial
19. True	19.	Rick Perry
20. True	20.	Samuel Lanham
21. True	21.	Executive Order
22. True	22.	Reduction
23. False	23.	State-of-the-State Message
24. False	24.	William Clements
25. False	25.	David Whitley
26. True		

CHAPTER NINE – The Judicial Branch of Texas Government

True/False Questions: Fill-in-the-Blank Questions:

1. False	1.	Common Law
2. False	2.	Civil Law
3. True	3.	Beyond a Reasonable Doubt
4. False	4.	*Furman v Georgia*
5. True	5.	*Ring v Arizona*

6. False		6.	Search Warrant
7. True		7.	Capital Offense
8. True		8.	Supreme Court/Court of Criminal Appeals
9. True		9.	Jury
10. False		10.	Plea Bargaining
11. True		11.	Exclusionary Rule
12. False		12.	*Illinois v Rodriguez*
13. False		13.	Statutory Law
14. False		14.	Tort Law
15. True		15.	Recidivism
16. True		16.	Criminal Law
17. True		17.	Change of Venue
18. False		18.	*Ruiz v Estelle*
19. False		19.	Jurisdiction
20. False		20.	Recognizance
21. True		21.	8th Amendment
22. False		22.	Administrative Law
23. False		23.	Court of Last Resort
24. True		24.	Injunction
25. True		25.	Law
26. False		26.	Texas Dept of Criminal Justice
27. False		27.	Constitutional Law
28. True		28.	Court of Criminal Appeals, Texas Supreme Court
29. True		29.	*Boykin v Alabama*
30. True		30.	Texas Department of Criminal Justice
31. False		31.	First Degree Felony
32. True		32.	*Boyd v United States*
33. False		33.	*Williams v Taylor*
34. False		34.	Bail
35. True		35.	Original Jurisdiction
36. False		36.	Political Question
37. False		37.	Indictment
38. True		38.	Pre-emptory Challenges

CHAPTER TEN– The Public Policy Process

True/False Questions: Fill-in-the-Blank Questions:

1. False		1.	Policy Output
2. True		2.	Mandates
3. False		3.	Problem
4. True		4.	Objectives
5. False		5.	Preventive
6. False		6.	Distributive Policies
7. True		7.	Privatization
8. True		8.	Dedicated Funding

9. False	9.	Impoundment
10. True	10.	Legislative Budgeting Board
11. True	11.	Tax
12. False	12.	Fiscal Policy
13. False	13.	Substantive Policies
14. True	14.	Policy
15. False	15.	License
16. True	16.	Alleviative
17. True	17.	Subsidies
18. True	18.	Earmarking
19. True	19.	Elasticity
20. True	20.	Zero-Based
21. False	21.	Deficit
22. False	22.	Budget
23. True	23.	Procedural Policies
24. True	24.	User Fees
25. False	25.	Public Policy
26. True	26.	Preventive Approach
27. False	27.	Line Item Veto
28. True	28.	Capital Expense

CHAPTER ELEVEN – Civil Rights and Civil Liberties

True/False Questions:

Fill-in-the-Blank Questions:

1. True	1.	*Gitlow v New York*
2. False	2.	Clear and Present Danger
3. False	3.	Contract Clause
4. False	4.	Civil Rights
5. True	5.	Superior/Inferior
6. False	6.	Blood Quantum
7. True	7.	Civil Rights Act
8. True	8.	W.E.B. DuBois
9. False	9.	19th Amendment
10. False	10.	Sharecropping
11. True	11.	Paternalistic Attitude
12. True	12.	Discrimination
13. False	13.	Elizabeth Cady Stanton
14. True	14.	Human Rights
15. False	15.	Establishment Clause
16. True	16.	Individual Liberty
17. False	17.	White Fear
18. True	18.	Restrictive Covenant
19. False	19.	13th Amendment
20. True	20.	Nativism
21. True	21.	Prejudice

22. False	22.	Procedural Due Process
23. False	23.	Symbolic Speech
24. False	24.	Child Benefit Theory
25. False	25.	Menger Eight
26. True	26.	*Barron v Baltimore*
27. True	27.	Mrs. A. J. Fey
28. False	28.	Eleanor Brackenridge
29. True	29.	David Molak
30. False	30.	Bill of Rights
31. False	31.	Judicial Review
32. False	32.	*Engle v Vitale*
33. True	33.	Pure Speech
34. True	34.	*New York Times v Sullivan*
35. False	35.	*New York Times v United States*
36. False	36.	Due Process
37. True	37.	Harriet Tubman
38. True	38.	14th/15th Amendments
39. True	39.	*Brown v Board of Education of Topeka, Kansas*
	40.	Manifest Destiny
	41.	Pink Collar

CHAPTER TWELVE – Social Service Public Policy Issues

True/False Questions:

Fill in the Blank Questions:

1. False	1.	Absolute Poverty
2. True	2.	Living Wage
3. False	3.	Section 8
4. True	4.	Colonias
5. False	5.	Almshouse
6. False	6.	*Fleming v Nestor*
7. False	7.	Family Support Act
8. False	8.	Food Stamp Program
9. False	9.	Medicaid
10. True	10.	Children's Health Insurance Program
11. False	11.	Unemployment Insurance
12. True	12.	Medicare
13. True	13.	Social Security Act
14. True	14.	Doughnut Hole
15. False	15.	Poverty
16. True	16.	Hyperpoor
17. True	17.	Supplemental Security Income
18. False	18.	Food Secure
19. False	19.	Temporary Assistance to Needy Families
20. True	20.	Means Tested
21. False	21.	Entitlements

CHAPTER THIRTEEN – Urban Governance and Public Policy Issues

True False Questions:

1. False
2. True
3. False
4. False
5. False
6. True
7. False
8. True
9. False
10. True
11. True
12. False
13. True
14. False
15. True
16. False
17. False
18. True
19. True
20. True
21. True
22. True
23. False
24. True
25. True
26. True
27. True

Fill-in-the-Blank Questions:

1. Homeowners Associations
2. Bedroom Cities
3. County/Special Districts
4. Mayor-Council
5. County Clerk
6. City-Council Consolidation
7. Commissioners' Court
8. Council-Manager
9. Initiative Petition
10. General Law Cities
11. Special District
12. Tax Assessor Collector
13. Strong-Mayor Council
14. Home Rule Cities
15. Annexation
16. Corporate Side
17. Dillon Rule
18. Ordinance
19. Commission
20. Central Business District
21. Weak-Mayor Council
22. City Charter
23. Home Rule Enabling Act
24. Extraterritorial Jurisdiction
25. Reservation
26. Incorporation
27. Weak-Mayor Council
28. Non-Renewable Goods
29. Tax Abatement
30. Zoning

CHAPTER FOURTEEN – The Politics of Highways and Transportation

True/False Questions:

1. False
2. True
3. False
4. False
5. True
6. False
7. True
8. True
9. False
10. False
11. False
12. False
13. True
14. False
15. True
16. True
17. False
18. False
19. True
20. True
21. True
22. False
23. False
24. True
25. False
26. True
27. False
28. True
29. True

Fill-in-the-Blank Questions:

1. Jackass Line
2. James Hogg
3. Department of Transportation
4. Texas Good Roads Association
5. Bus Lane
6. Federal Aid Highway Act
7. Para Transit Fleets
8. Demanding Ethics, Responsibility and Accountability in Legislation
9. Stop the Banks and the Railroads
10. Texas Department of Transportation
11. Bureau of Public Roads
12. Stop-and-Ride Buses
13. Deficient Bridge
14. Highway Beautification Act
15. Kings Highway
16. Interstate Commerce Clause
17. Works Progress Administration
18. Pay-as-You-Go
19. High Occupancy Vehicle Lane
20. Transguide
21. Dedicated Fund
22. Housing and Urban Development
23. Highway Department
24. Highway Lobby
25. Land Grant Law

CHAPTER FIFTEEN – Education Policy in Texas

True/False Questions:

1. False
2. True
3. True
4. False
5. False

Fill-in-the-Blank Questions:

1. Smith Hughes Act
2. Elementary School Act
3. No Child Left Behind
4. Common Schools
5. Gilmer-Aiken School Laws

6. False	6. No Pass, No Play
7. True	7. State Board of Education
8. True	8. Texas Assessment of Academic Skills
9. False	9. Dropout
10. True	10. Enrichment Money
11. True	11. *San Antonio Independent School District v Rodriguez*
12. False	12. Textbook Selection Committee
13. True	13. Common Districts
14. True	14. Pell Grant
15. False	15. Northwest Ordinance
16. False	16. Voucher Program
17. False	17. Ad Valorem
18. False	18. Completion Rates
19. True	19. Economically Disadvantaged Student
20. True	20. Independent School Districts
21. True	21. Select Committee for Public Education
22. True	22. American Recovery and Reinvestment Act
23. False	23. *A Nation at Risk*
24. True	24. Lyndon Johnson
25. True	25. GI Bill of Rights
	26. Serviceman's Readjustment Act
	27. Texas Education Agency
	28. Robinhood

CHAPTER SIXTEEN – Texans and Their Environment

True/False Questions:

Fill-in-the-Blank Questions:

1. False	1. National Ambient Air Quality Standards
2. True	2. Pollution
3. True	3. Water
4. False	4. Edwards
5. False	5. Air Pollution
6. False	6. CFC
7. False	7. Solid Waste
8. False	8. Superfund
9. True	9. Wilderness
10. False	10. Municipal Solid Waste
11. True	11. Suspended Particulates
12. False	12. Wetlands
13. True	13. Estuary
14. True	14. Point Source
15. True	15. Sierra Club
16. True	16. Water Pollution
17. False	17. Coastal Zone

18. True
19. False
20. True
21. True
22. False
23. True
24. False
25. True
26. True

18. Smog
19. Air
20. Acre Foot
21. Drinking Water
22. Waste
23. Non-point Source
24. Impact Statement
25. Pelican Island
26. Non-Attainment
27. Safe Drinking Water Act
28. Biochemical Oxygen Demand